Cemetery Inscriptions, and Revolutionary, War of 1812, and Civil War Veterans of Bowdoin, Maine

by

Charlene B. Bartlett

and

Jayne E. Bickford

HERITAGE BOOKS
2012

HERITAGE BOOKS
AN IMPRINT OF HERITAGE BOOKS, INC.

Books, CDs, and more—Worldwide

For our listing of thousands of titles see our website
at
www.HeritageBooks.com

Published 2012 by
HERITAGE BOOKS, INC.
Publishing Division
100 Railroad Ave. #104
Westminster, Maryland 21157

Copyright © 1993 Charlene B. Bartlett and Jayne E. Bickford

Other Heritage Books by Charlene B. Bartlett and Jayne E. Bickford:
*Cemetery Inscriptions, and Revolutionary, War of 1812,
and Civil War Veterans of Bowdoin, Maine*
*CD: Cemetery Inscriptions, and Revolutionary, War of 1812,
and Civil War Veterans of Bowdoin, Maine*

Other Heritage Books by Jayne E. Bickford:
Early Bowdoin, Maine Families and Some of Their Descendants
Watkins: A Beginning Genealogy, Volumes 1–2

All rights reserved. No part of this book may be reproduced or transmitted in any form or by any means, electronic or mechanical, including photocopying, recording or by any information storage and retrieval system without written permission from the author, except for the inclusion of brief quotations in a review.

International Standard Book Numbers
Paperbound: 978-1-55613-771-6
Clothbound: 978-0-7884-3449-5

TABLE OF CONTENTS

Introduction	v
South Cemetery	1
Hix Small Cemetery	19
West Bowdoin Cemetery	27
Woodlawn Cemetery	61
North Cemetery	78
Millay Cemetery	87
Adams Cemetery	95
Brown Cemetery	102
Allen Family Cemetery	104
Skelton Family Cenetery	104
White Cemetery	105
Leonard Family Cenetery	110
Temple/Randall Cemetery	110
Wheeler Family Cemetery	113
Buker Cemetery	115
Niles Cemetery	116
Ward Cemetery	118
Town Grant Cemetery	119
Campbell Cemetery	120
Gowell Cemetery	121
Gowell Burial Ground	121
Buker Allen Cemetery	122
Bickford Burial Ground	122
Jones Cemetery	122
Grover Cemetery	123
Lewis Cemetery	123
Foster Burial Lot	124
Small Cemetery	124
Grover Cemetery	125
Williams Family Cemetery	126
Humphrey Purinton Burial Lot	127
Bubier-Cripps Cemetery	127
Jacques Cemetery	127
Ephraim Small Cemetery	130
Thomas Skelton Family Cemetery	131
Elliott Cemetery	131

Nelson Family Lot	135
Emery Purinton Farm Cemetery	135
Carr Cemetery	137
Cornish or Gully Woods Cemetery	140
Thompson Cemetery	142
Rogers Family Cemetery	143
Bradford Haskell Cemetery	143
Jack Cemetery	144
Potter Cemetery	145
Day Burial Lot	146
Revolutionary War Veterans	147
War of 1812 Veterans	150
Civil War Veterans	152
Addendum	160

INTRODUCTION

In the early 1970's my friend Jayne Bickford and I joined the Maine Old Cemetery Association (MOCA). Being involved in genealogy, we were captivated by its aim of collecting all Maine cemetery inscriptions and making these inscriptions accessible to all interested researchers. In a haze of enthusiastic naivete, we thought largely of the six readily apparent cemeteries in Bowdoin and volunteered.

We never dreamed that over the course of twenty years, we would climb hills, push through brush, wade brooks and fight black flies. These efforts, plus research, have netted us inscriptions from 45 Bowdoin, Maine, cemeteries, plus those from the Potter Cemetery, which is across the town line in Lisbon, but which was once a part of Bowdoin. This cemetery is in such bad condition that we feel compelled to include these inscriptions to get them on record.

Settlers started moving into the area that is now Bowdoin, Maine, in the 1750's. The area was incorporated into a town in 1788, and in 1799 the portion that was to become present-day Lisbon, Lisbon Center, Lisbon Falls and Sabattus (once Webster) split off to incorporate as the Town of Thompsonborough.

Though Bowdoin has always been a small town, through the years many people who lived in Bowdoin have moved on to other areas, and their descendants are often searching information concerning their ancestors. Bowdoin still has the earliest book of vital records, but in 1872 all other vital records were burned in a fire that took Emerson's store. For the next 20 years vital records were apparently not kept; so official records, with the exception of the one very early book, are not available until those for 1892. Thus, these cemetery inscriptions appear to be the most complete vital records available for Bowdoin.

Rachel Townsend Cox edited the <u>Vital Records of Bowdoin, Maine to the Year 1892</u>, and had them printed in three volumes in 1945. Her information does not come from the Town of Bowdoin vital records, except for some data from the first record book started in 1788. Mrs. Cox took her information from census records, some cemetery records, old newspapers, and from old family records and Bibles which are no longer available. This is an invaluable effort, but in no way contains a complete enumeration of all Bowdoin cemeteries or families, and Mrs. Cox made no attempt to give the location of the cemeteries which she did include. It is not known what criteria she used, but it is apparent that, in many cases, her death records include more data than was on the stones.

In 1967 Mrs. Doris M. Rowland of Bath, Maine, compiled and had printed a limited number of the <u>Death Records of Bowdoinham, Maine</u>. She included a few inscriptions from Bowdoin cemeteries, and in a few cases her records have given us a date or name which was illegible or missing when we copied the inscriptions.

We have also referred to the 1850 Census for Bowdoin, which we copied from microfilm, for verification of some names and ages. Another source, particularly helpful when listing the veterans of the Revolutionary, 1812 and Civil Wars, was the Bowdoin Selectmen's records. These records give the veteran's name, service record, birth and death dates, and the next of kin. The records were made many years ago to guide the Selectmen in placing Memorial Day flags. These cards are in no way complete, but do give some valuable data not available elsewhere.

In the case of the North, Jacques and Emery Purinton Farm Cemeteries, we were given copies of inscriptions copied at least 50 years ago. These copies listed some inscriptions no longer legible and even some from stones no longer to be found, and this information has been included in this book.

In 1991, with the information from 46 cemeteries copied, it seemed important to us that this data be published in book form and made available to others, as the information about many of these Bowdoin people is not available from any other source. Many of the cemeteries are quite inaccessible and the stones are rapidly deteriorating. Over a 20-year span, since we started copying these inscriptions, we have discovered that some of those first copied in 1972 are either no longer legible or the stones are missing. This points to the need for this material to be published and made available to all before more of the inscriptions are irrevocably lost.

Irrovacably lost, of course, are the names of those persons whose graves are marked only with field stones, and there could be more burial lots than we are aware of, for on 27 July 1992, the Lewiston paper stated, "Gravel pit yields human remains." A piece of wood and a plate such as put on caskets at one time were also found, and it is assumed that the skull found by a man walking his dog and other bones found later are from a family burial ground unknown to us at this time.

We have copied inscriptions, proofread the typed copies, and then proofread the entire manuscript trying conscientiously for perfection. However, as in all human endeavors there may be some errors. We have in some instances even returned to a cemetery to double check data, but if you have ever copied old stones you know the difficulties of deciding if the worn and lichen covered number is a "1," a "4," or a "7."

Epitaphs have been included if they were unusual or if the inscribed thoughts were especially poignant. If we have included additional helpful information, not found on the stone, we have put that information in parenthesis. We have carefully used original spellings of names and in many cases the spelling of the names has varied on the same burial lot.

We thank the many people who have helped us with this project, the outdoorsmen who have told us of obscure cemeteries, particularly Leon Skelton who took us to one of these cemeteries in his four-wheel drive truck. Thanks go to June Wheeler and Doris Gagne who took us into the woods to the White Cemetery that we had searched for so long in vain. Thanks to Leah (Letourneau) Smith, who has a never ending interest in Bowdoin cemeteries, and who has carefully drawn a map of Bowdoin, indicating the locations of cemeteries and has taken us to some of these cemeteries. One memorable spring day Leah took us to the Buker and Niles family cemeteries up on Haigh Mountain. The Bowdoin Historical Society's members have supported us in our desire to copy and record inscriptions and to preserve them for their genealogical and historical value. We are grateful to many people - some not specifically named - who have helped us make this collection of cemetery inscriptions more complete, and who have helped in so many ways to make this book possible.

We sincerely hope that this book will be of considerable assistance to those persons seeking their Bowdoin, Maine, roots.

                                        Charlene B. Bartlett

Charlene B. Bartlett   Jayne E. Bickford
3 Avery Street   RFD#1, Box 1280
Lisbon Falls, ME 04252   Lisbon Falls, ME 04252

South Cemetery - located approximately 1½ miles from Bowdoin Center on a road off from the Meadow Road. At one time South Church was opposite the cemetery. This was built in 1836 and torn down in the early 1960's. A new church has been built and was first used in December of 1991. The inscriptions were copied during the summers of 1972, 1973 and 1992. Some updating was also done in 1992. See addendum.

SHAW, Lionel B. - born 27 Jul 1883, died 15 Nov 1927.
  Statira C. Harvey - wife of Lionel B. Shaw, born 29 Jul 1890, died 24 Jun 1953.
  Baby Son of Lionel B. & Satira C. Shaw - (no dates).

GILPATRICK, Ida M. - born 8 Jul 1885, died 13 Jul 1924 (stone shows Ida M. Shaw wife of Edmond H. Gilpatrick).

BICKFORD, Our Baby Robert C. - 1936-1936 (child of Robert C. and Cynthia (Durgin) Bickford, grandson of Robert H. and Edna B. (Wellman) Bickford).
  Robert H. - 1880-1960.
  Edna B. - 1873-1961.
  Earl W. - 1906-1929 (son of Robert H. and Edna B.).

SETTLE, John W. - 1874-1941.
  Mary C. F. - his wife, 1872-1958.
  Baby Barbara - (no dates).

CURTIS, Evelyn P. - wife of Norman E. Curtis, 1873-1933.

COOMBS, George L. - 1854-1937.
  Nancy E. - his wife, 1861-1941.
  Robert G. - 1895-1951.

JONES, George D. - 1856-1938.
  Marcia O. - his wife, 1866-1955.

BARTLETT, Margaret - dau of G. D. & M. O. Jones, 1902-1952.

   Raymond H. - husband, 1893-1942.
ESTES, Mary J. - mother, 1898-1987.
  David D. - 1896-1969.
SKELTON, Morris J. - 3 Oct 1897-9 May 1957.
GODDARD, Robert R. - husband, 1888-1964.
  Edith A. - his wife, 1893-1962.
HARRINGTON, Marie - 1963-1963 (funeral director's marker only).
HITINGLEY, Arthur - 1865-1937.
MASON, Charles Digby - son of Rev. & Mrs. Paul S. Mason, 1951-1962.
WEBBER, Arthur E. - 1914-
  Marion L. - 1914-1965.
McIVER, Herbert E. - 1921-1934.
  Huldah H. - 1897-1961, wife.
  Edward D. - 1899-1968, husband.
CORNISH, Elizabeth - 1907-1973.
  Roland W. - 1907-1970.
  Mary Anna - 1929-
SHAW, Enoch Y. - 4 Oct 1852-18 Feb 1926.
  Carrie C. Chandler - his wife, 31 Mar 1852-15 Sep 1942.
PROUT, Herbert L. -
  Emma J. Potter - his wife, 1887-1909.
ROGERS, Roland E. - 5 Jul 1844-18 Oct 1911.
  Fannie D. Campbell - his wife, 24 Jun 1844-27 Aug 1969.
  M. E. C. - (no dates, marker only).
  James E. - 9 Apr 1866-16 Feb 1906.
UTECHT, Edward A. - 1920-1932 (Boy Scout marker & symbol)
  In Memoriam
  Edward A. Utecht
  Brunswick, Maine
  Tenderfoot Troop 32
  Born March 9, 1920
  Died December 24, 1932
MARSDEN, Ethel L. - 1881-1912.

Emma J. -

LEWIS, Ruth L. - 1841-1914 (on Marsden lot).

GIVEN, Charity A. - 1834-1914 (on Augusta Adams lot).

ADAMS, Augusta M. - 1845-1920.

SMALL, Sewell E. - died 23 Jan 1915 at 88 yrs.
   Abbie - wife of Sewall Small, died 28 Feb 1861 at 28 yrs (on Sewall's stone spelled "Sewell.")
   Mary - wife of Elisha Small, died 15 Feb 1859 at 55 yrs. 1 m.
   Elisha, Capt. - died 17 Feb 1872 at 73 yrs. 2 m.

TRUFANT, Charles E. - 1870-1931.
   Daisy D. Spencer - his wife, 1875-1916.

SPENCER, Richard W. - 1821-1906.
   Rebecca J. Plummer - his wife, 1837-1927.

LEONARD, Isaac - 1834-1926.
   Nancy Jane - his wife, 1840-1917.
   Nancy J. - (no dates).
   G. Alton - (no dates).

SKELTON, Thomas W. - 1845-1918.
   Mary L. Holbrock - his wife, 1849-1925.
   Linwood T. - 1872-1957.
   Lena M. Allard - his wife, 1878-1968.

ROY, Charlotte D. - dau, 9 Mar 1919-19 Nov 1919.
   Arthur J. - 1894-1955.
   Gladys M. - 1893-1960.

CALL, Charlotte M. - mother, 29 Mar 1874-3 Jun 1933 (on Roy lot).

PIERCE, Franklin - 1874-1923 (Knights of Pythias FCB No. 42 Maint emblem).
   Adeline M. - his wife, 1882-1945.

McIVER, William - 1850-1921.
   Annie C. - his wife, 1859-1935.
   Alfred C. - 12 Mar 1878-13 Jan 1964, Pvt US Marine Corps Spanish American War.

ADAMS, Edwin S. - 25 Apr 1890-28 Sep 1959.

Mabel Ada Wilson - his wife, 22 Feb 1897-21 Feb 1924.
  Gerald E., Jr. - 19 Sep 1945-14 Apr 1946.
  Laurence T., Jr. - Inf, 1954 (son of Laurence and Geneva Adams).
  Nathan E. - 1861-1940.
  Margaret A. Trufant - his wife, 1865-1952.
  Clyde T. - 1902- .
  Blanche E. Mitchell - his wife, 1898- .
WILSON, Irving E. - 1879-1961.
  Edythe L. Adams - his wife, 1883-1962.
  Bernard E. - their son, 1905-1964.
SMALL, Arthur L. - 1889-1933.
  Sarah L. - his wife, 1897-1988.
  Timothy N. - 24 May 1875 (5 ?)-2 Feb 1946.
JOYCE, Stella Small - 20 Nov 1884-19 Nov 1956.
GOODRIDGE, Horace E. - 1902-1983.
  Zepha L. - wife, 1888-1957.
SMALL, Olive - 1878-1969 (on Goodrich lot).
  Joseph Alverna - 1885-1963.
  Carrie Estelle - 1894-1960.
HAWKES, Martha J. Huntington - 1832-1918.
  Mary M. - 1866-1866.
HUNTINGTON, Margaret - dau of J. & T. Huntington, died 14 Mar 1850 at 8 m.
  Thirzaett - wife of James Huntington, died 10 Oct 1850 at 23 yrs. 9 m.
  James - died 21 Dec 1860 at 42 yrs.
POTTER, Joseph C. - son of Alden & Charlotte Potter, died 4 Mar 1856 at 10 yrs. 5 m.
  James Carr - son of Alden & Charlotte Potter, died 26 Aug 1838 at 3 yrs. 7 m.
  Charlotte C. - wife of Alden Potter, died 7 Dec 1868 at 56 yrs. 2 m.
  Alden - died 14 Mar 1876 at 65 yrs. 7 m.
MERRILL, Charles W. - died 8 Dec 1878 at 61 yrs. 6 m.

HANSON, Tabitha P. - wife of Jacob and dau of Luther & Priscilla Hall, died 22 Apr 1869 at 49 yrs. 8 m. 9 d.
HALL, Christiana - wife of Luther Hall, died 15 Jan 1815 at 24 yrs.
   Priscilla - wife of Luther Hall, died 28 Nov 1860 at 65 yrs. 8 m.
   Luther, Esq. - died 9 Dec 1878 at 89 yrs. 4 m.
COTTON, Isaac H. - born 21 Jul 1811, died 23 Mar 1888.
   Rhoda L. - his wife, born 11 Jul 1813, died 17 Feb 1891.
   Clara A. - dau of I. H. & R. L. Cotton, died 6 Dec 1865 at 20 yrs. 10 m.
   Isaac H., Capt. - died 3 Sep 1843 at 76 yrs.
   Elizabeth S. - his wife, died 3 Jan 1841 at 64 yrs. 6 m.
JAQUES, Stafford - died 22 Oct 1877 at 71 yrs. 3 m.
   Harriet - wife of Stafford Jaques, died 4 Jan 1872 at 67 yrs. 10 m.
   Horace - died 23 Jan 1842 at 4 yrs. 9 m.
   Harriet E. - died 8 Sep 1840 at 11 m. 14 d. Children of Stafford & Harriet Jaques.
POTTER, Hannah - relict of Joseph Potter, Esq., died 15 Feb 1850 at 76 yrs.
   Joseph, Esq. - died 9 May 1831 at 56 yrs. 1 m.
MERRIMAN, John - died 8 Apr 1855 at 23 yrs. 4 m. 9 d.
HINKLEY, Thomas T. - died 31 Jul 1894 at 76 yrs.
   Mary E. - wife of Thos. T. Hinkley, died 2 Sep 1891 at 67 yrs.
ALEXANDER, Elizabeth - wife of Capt. James Alexander, died 21 Jul 1857 at 72 yrs.
   James, Capt. - died 27 Oct 1856 at 69 yrs.
POTTER, Chas., Esq. - died 16 Dec 1846 at 74 yrs. Erected by C. Purington.

Louisa - dau of Charles & Abigail Potter,
who departed this life 2 Dec 1842 at 33 yrs.
HILTON, Mary E. - died 15 Jun 1849 at 21 yrs.
(1 field stone).
DENHAM, Thomas - died 19 Nov 1799 at 34 yrs.
Catharine - his wife, died 17 Apr 1844 at 74
yrs.
POTTER, John - died 10 Dec 1855 at 89 yrs. 4 m.
James, Eld. - for 23 years Pastor of the first
Baptist Church in Bowdoin, died 22 Mar 1815,
at 81 yrs. 1 m.
Mary - his wife, died 22 Jul 1822 at 83 yrs.
MERRYMAN, Bailey - born 1798, died 1858.
Mary W. - his wife, 9 Dec 1807-7 Dec 1896.
Geo. H. - died 28 Mar 1841 at 19 m.
Inf dau - died 13 Feb 1844 - children of B.
& M. Merryman.
ADAMS, Mary Jane - dau of James & Sarah Adams,
died 6 Aug 1842 at 25 yrs. 4 m.
WICKWIRE, Mary - aged 67 yrs. (no dates).
RHODES, Julia S. - wife of Christopher Rhodes,
died 29 Jul 1851 at 27 yrs. 10 m.
CARR, Martha - mother, wife of Daniel Carr,
died 20 Apr 1880 at 79 yrs. 4 m.
(There are two stones down in this area and
not readable.)
Daniel - father, died 21 Jul 1956 at 57 yrs.
2 m.
Mary Eastman - wife of Joseph Carr, Esq.,
died 14 Feb 1849 at 80 yrs. 8 m.
Joseph, Esq. - died 3 Apr 1850 at 84 yrs. 8 m.
CONNOR, Mrs. Martha - wife of Simon Connor, died
24 Jun 1826 at 52 yrs.
Martha - wife of Simon Connor, died 16 Dec
1808 at 38 yrs.
Arthur - son of Simon & Martha Connor, died
Jul 1804 at 2 yrs. (no day).
Simon, Dea. - died 2 Aug 1842 at 72 yrs.

Mary, Mrs. - wife of Simon Connor, died 14 Apr 1797 at 28 yrs.

ALEXANDER, Albert E. - died 30 Aug 1847 at 17 yrs.
 Hacker - died 5 Feb 1846 at 22 yrs.
 Sons of Wm. & Lucy Alexander.
 Daniel H. - son of Wm. & Lucy Alexander, died 3 Dec 1847 at 22 yrs.
 William - died 28 May 1846 (no age).

ADAMS, Samual A. - died 15 Jan 1891 at 74 yrs. 4 m.
 Minerva S. - his wife, died 20 Feb 1914 at 91 yrs. 5 m.
 Henry - died 15 Jan 1888 at 74 yrs.
 Saml. C. - died 4 Aug 1913 at 62 yrs. 6 m.
 David A., Col. - died 15 Mar 1839 at 38 yrs. 5 m. (American flag).
 Nathan - died 1 Sep 1855 at 81 yrs. 5 m.
 Martha - his wife, died 28 Mar 1849 at 75 yrs. 3 m.

MERRIMAN, Katy - dau of Skolfield & Submit Merriman, died 23 Jun 1868 at 25 yrs.

ELLIOT, John P. - died 4 Nov 1841 at 15 yrs.
 Joseph - died 1 Feb 1832 at 10 yrs., son of Joseph & C. Elliot.

BRIMIGION, Wm. - died 17 Sep 1856 at 49 yrs.

MERRYMAN, Submit - wife of Skolfield Merryman, died 13 Dec 1879 at 59 yrs. 2 m.
 Skolfield - died 27 Apr 1846 at 30 yrs. 8 m.

ELLIOT, Catherine, Mrs. - wife of Capt. Joseph Elliot, died 11 Apr 1831 at 34 yrs.
 Isaac - died 5 Sep 1828 at 5 m.
 Josephine - died 3 Nov 1830 at 4 m.
 Joseph - died 29 Aug 1850 at 50 yrs.

POTTER, Charles L. - 1851-1920.
 Allena Nellie Chapin - his wife, 1858-1925.

FARMER, Addie A. - 1856-1924 (sister to Allena).

BOWERS, James L. - died 1 Jun 1867 at 47 yrs. 11 m.

Mary P. - wife of James L. Bowers, died 6 May 1890 at 68 yrs. 9 m.
Mary E. - died 2 Oct 1920 at 69 yrs. 11 m.
Clementine H. - died 20 Sep 1923 at 71 yrs.

HOGAN, A. J. - born 3 Dec 1819, died 9 Jun 1873.
Jane H. - his wife, born 28 Mar 1827, died 12 Jan 1915.

BROWN, Alpheus M. - 1847-1916 (Knights of Pythias flag).
Eleona A. - his wife, 1851-1914.
Robert A. - 1874-   .
Their Children
Robert A. - 1908-1909.
Charles R. - 1913-1914.
Alpheus M. - 1911-   .
Emma M. - wife of Robert A. Brown, 1874-1913.
Robert Alpheus - son of R. A. & E. M. Brown, 1908-1909.

POTTER, D. Emery - father, 1839-1929.
E. Jane Adams - mother, his wife, 1844-1913.
Minnie A. - dau of D. E. & L. J. Potter, died 16 Mar 1888 at 3 yrs. 7 m.
Rebecca G. - dau of Stephen & Margaret Potter, died 2 Jul 1874 at 33 yrs. 3 m.
Margaret - wife of Stephen Potter, died 13 Nov 1891 at 88 yrs. 7 m.
Stephen - died 14 Nov 1873 at 85 yrs. 5 m.

STAPLES, Alden - died 18 Nov 1908 at 93 yrs. 9 m.
Eliza - wife of Alden Staples, died 7 Apr 1883 at 64 yrs.
Geo. H. - 1857-1920.
Harriot Hawthorne - wife, 1858-1936.

SMALL, Frank W. - 1864-1895.
Robert H. - 1872-1901.
Vilettie - dau of J. & A. Small, died 17 Mar 1886 at 17 yrs. 11 m.
Joel - Co. F. 24 ME Inf., 1837-1900.

CARTER, Josie E. - dau of Wm. S. & Abbie H.
  Carter, died 12 Oct 1887 at 18 yrs. 9 m.
  Alice M. - dau of Wm. S. & Abbie H. Carter,
  died 23 Jun 1883 at 15 yrs. 11 m.
  William S. - died 22 Jan 1892 at 45 yrs.
JAQUES, Daniel S. - 1833-1923.
  Ruth Abbie - his wife, 1835-1926.
  Isaac - died 11 Sep 1858 at 56 yrs.
  Hannah L. - his wife, died 13 Dec 1900 at 91 yrs.
  Lovina A. - their dau, died 9 Oct 1847 at 3 yrs.
POTTER, George - 1832-1888.
COOMBS, J. Colby - 1839-1884 (on George Potter stone).
ROGERS, James L. - died 16 Mar 1896 at 82 yrs. 7 m.
  Mary E. - his wife, died 24 Feb 1858 at 36 yrs. 7 m.
  Matilda E. - his wife, died 3 May 1916 at 88 yrs. 1 m.
  Mary A. - dau of James L. and Mary E. Rogers, died 6 Aug 1851 at 11 yrs. 4 m.
  James W. - 1859-1923.
  Grant - 1868-1933.
  Susie E. - his wife, 1870-1948.
ALLEN, Everett L. - 1865-1940.
  Eben T. - 1872-1930.
  Edwin T. - born & died 1895.
  Ivory T. - 4 Feb 1836-26 May 1900.
  Isabella S. - his wife, 14 Aug 1846- 1 May 1914.
POLLEY, George R. - 14 Nov 1857-13 Dec 1914.
  Lydia Carr - his wife, 11 Jan 1861-23 Nov 1928.
McLEAN, Mabel Emma Polley - their dau, wife of Arthur McLean, 31 May 1900-22 Jul 1920 (on Polley stone).

RIDEOUT, John P. - 1832-1911.
　Elizabeth P. - wife of John P. Rideout, died
　19 Jun 1863 at 31 yrs. 3 m.
　Naomi W. - wife of John P. Rideout, 1844-1917.
SYLVESTER, Edmund - son of Rufus & Ann H.
　Sylvester, died 27 Aug 1850 at 4 yrs. 10 m.
　Emily - dau of Rufus & Ann H. Sylvester, died
　2 Aug 1838 at 11 m.
　Inf. son of Rufus & Ann H. Sylvester, died 4
　Oct 1829 at 1 m. 9 d.
　Mary - dau of Rufus & Ann H. Sylvester, died
　2 Feb 1850 at 19 yrs. 2 m.
　Rufus - 25 Jun 1803-21 Oct 1884.
　Anna H. - his wife, 30 Nov 1806-21 Aug 1896.
　Mary - 2 Dec 1830-2 Feb 1850.
　Edmund - 15 Sep 1852-22 Apr 1853.
　Emilie H. - dau of R. & A. Sylvester, 2 Jul
　1839-4 May 1910.
　Inf. son - 25 Aug 1829-4 Oct 1829.
　Emily - 10 Sep 1837-2 Aug 1838.
　Edmund H. - 6 Oct 1845-27 Aug 1850.
WHITTEMORE, Elizabeth C. Sylvester, wife of
　Warren B. Whittemore & dau of Rufus & Anna H.
　Sylvester, born in Bowdoin 8 Nov 1841, died
　in Lisbon 25 Aug 1890.
　Warren B. - 23 Nov 1838-27 Apr 1906. A
　pioneer settler of Fort Bidwell California,
　and a resident in that vicinity for 48 years.
THOMPSON, William H. - died 6 Oct 1863 at 19 yrs.
　A member of the 1st ME Cavalry, served a year
　and a half and was honorably discharged.
　George A. - died 14 Feb 1864 at 20 yrs.
　Sons of Abel & Julia Thompson.
　Thankful P. - wife of Dea. Abijah Thompson,
　died 5 Jun 1864 at 65 yrs.
　Abijah, Dea. - died 23 Jul 1863 at 77 yrs.
　4 m.
　Rachel - wife of Abijah Thompson, Esq., died

13 Mar 1853 at 70 yrs. 8 m.
Minerva H. A., Mrs. - wife of Capt. Nathan T.
Thompson, died 10 Mar 1847 at 26 yrs.
This humble stone erected by her bereaved Husband who but a few months since led her to the Hymenal Altar.
Nathan T., Capt. - aged 43 yrs. & 6 m. of Ship Wm. M. Rogers which perished at sea on her passage from Liverpool to New York 21 Jun 1857.
POTTER, Elisha - died 26 Dec 1893 at 89 yrs. 11 m.
Eliza - wife of Elisha Potter, died 14 Feb 1884 at 78 yrs.
Eliza - died 15 Jul 1836 at 2 yrs.
Samuel A. - died 11 Sep 1840 at 4 yrs.
Alma E. - died 7 Oct 1841 at 3 yrs.
Children of Elisha & Eliza Potter.
Phebe - died 13 Oct 1841 at 8 m.
Winfield S. - died 10 Dec 1849 at 2 yrs.
Martha E. - died 7 May 1880 at 35 yrs.
Children of Elisha & Eliza Potter.
Emeline - dau of Elijah & Elixabeth Potter, died 12 Oct 1849 at 1 yr. 6 m. 13 d.
Hannah - dau of Elijah and Elizabeth Potter, died 15 Oct 1841 at 13 m.
CARR, Alfred - my husband died 13 Dec 1875 at 68 yrs. 3 m.
Mary P. - wife of Alfred Carr, died 23 Feb 1901 at 83 yrs. 5 m.
SMITH, Henrietta M. Hall - wife of Colby Smith, died 11 Jul 1902 at 26 yrs. 6 m. 11 d.
HALL, Harry - son of D. & L. E. Hall, died 28 Jun 1865 at 3 d.
Amanda E. - mother, wife of Denham Hall, died 30 Jul 1901 at 61 yrs.
Denham - died 2 May 1900 at 62 yrs.
Lydia E. - wife of Denham Hall, died 9 Oct 1865 at 33 yrs. 10 m.

MERRIMAN, Benj. A. - 20 Oct 1828-26 Jan 1910.
  Abbie E. - his wife, 23 Sep 1828-5 Jan 1909.
  Alice M. - 15 Nov 1864-8 Feb 1866.
  Helen - 23 Jan 1857-29 Mar 1889.
  Abbie - 2 Mar 1870-5 Mar 1870.
  Children of B. A. & A. E. Merriman.
COLBY, Samuel - 9 Jul 1803-19 Nov 1875.
  Mary M. - his wife, 19 Jul 1808-25 Dec 1889.
  Lieut. O. R. - 6 Aug 1834-13 Jun 1865.
SMALL, Nathaniel - 1798-1871.
  Hannah - his wife, 1798-1872.
  Joseph - 1844-1923.
  Zephalinda - his wife, 1847-1888.
MERRYMAN, Timothy, Jr. - died 30 Apr 1903 at 71 yrs. 11 m.
  Emma F. - wife of Timothy Merryman, Jr. - died 27 Apr 1881 at 40 yrs. 11 m.
  Appaann - wife of Capt. Timothy Merryman, died 11 Jan 1877 at 76 yrs. 9 m. 19 d.
  Timothy, Capt. - died 18 Jun 1874 at 74 yrs. 10 m. 27 d.
ALEXANDER, John H. - 1804-1880.
  Louisa M. - his wife, 1808-1886.
  D. Franklin - 1845-1909.
  Minerva T. - his wife, 1846-1911.
  Perley M. - their son, 1882-1883.
  Howard F. L. - 1886-1900.
  Abner P. - 1841-1878. Died in Oakland, Cal.
CARR, John H. - 1845-1896.
  Almira L. - his wife, 1847-1911.
  Octavia S. - 1843-1901.
  Rachel T. - 1838-1905.
ALEXANDER, John L. - 1843-1928.
  Annie L. - his wife, 1844-1926.
SMITH, Anna Laura (Vesey) - unmarked grave.
  (In 1972/73 the then superintendent of S. Cem. Robert Card said the grave was that of June Smith's mother. Bowdoin Town Report for Year

Ending 10 Feb 1936 shows Mrs. Smith d. 19 May 1935 at 89 yrs. 9 m. 11 d. A local resident says she was known as "Annie Laurie."

SMALL, Geo. W. - father, died 1 Jan 1917 at 82 yrs. 4 m.
  Rachel P. - mother, wife of Geo. W. Small, died 30 May 1892 at 55 yrs. 5 m.
  George S. - son of Geo. W. & Rachel P. Small, died 26 Jul 1887 at 21 yrs. 6 m.

MARSH, Nancy J. - wife of Charles A. Marsh died 23 Feb 1887 at 29 yrs. 6 m.

MOSELEY, Charles G. - 1849-1926.
  Abbie C. - his wife, 1853-1921.
  Mary E. - 1841-1890.
  Martha E. - 1843-1926.
  Fred S. C. - 1887-1967.

KENDRICK, Mabel F. - 1877-1917.

GOWELL, Alfred - 1805-1865.
  Elizabeth Brown - 1811-1892.
  William Morrill - 1849-1880.
  Gilbert M. - 1845-1908.
  Ella Cary - his wife, 1849-1906.

CURRIER, Ellen T. - mother, wife of Frank M. Currier, 1868-1896.
  Ellen S. - a dau, 1895-1896.

HUNTINGTON, Mary - wife of Benj. J. Huntington, died 26 Mar 1880 at 25 yrs. 10 m. 10 d.

TRUFANT, William W. - son of Wm. B. & Margaret A. Trufant, died 27 Jan 1877 at 13 yrs. 5 m. 22 d.
  William B. - 1830-1905.
  Margaret A. - his wife, 1836-1920.

WHITE, Minnie M. - wife of Melvin S. White, 16 Jul 1859-25 Nov 1935.

MARSHALL, Mason H. - 1835-1895, Corp. Co. H. 23rd ME Reg't Civil War.
  Ellen B. - his wife, 1839-1904.
  Mason H. - 1896-1972.

Carmalene L. - 1898-1982.
CORNISH, Charles - died 14 May 1850 at 50 yrs.
  Hannah - wife of Charles Cornish, died 29 Oct 1840 at 35 yrs.
PENNELL, Joshua - died 8 Feb 1861 at 78 yrs. 6 m.
  Susan - wife of Joshua Pennell, died 27 Apr 1875 at 77 yrs. 5 m.
HALL, Stephen W. - son of Isaac R. & Emeline P. Hall, died 16 Aug 1869 at 20 yrs. 10 m.
  Isaac R. - died 24 Mar 1900 at 88 yrs. 7 m. 15 d.
  Emeline P. - died 11 Nov 1899 at 82 yrs. 10 m. 15 d.
PLUMMER, Lovina O. - "Aunt Lovina" at top, died 20 Nov 1902 at 75 yrs.
  Nathaniel - died 14 Sep 1868 at 82 yrs. 7 m.
  Agnes - wife of Nathaniel Plummer, died 26 Apr 1873 at 85 yrs. 3 m.
HALL, Sarah P. - wife of Joseph Hall, died 22 Nov 1878 at 60 yrs. 5 m.
PLUMMER, Andrew - father, died 15 Oct 1899 at 77 yrs. 5 m.
  Elizabeth H. - mother, wife of Andrew Plummer, died 18 Mar 1892 at 63 yrs. 6 m.
NICHOLS, Benjamin - 20 Jan 1780-6 Mar 1859.
  Betsey - his wife, 21 Mar 1784-27 Oct 1847.
  Mary Ann - dau of Benj. & Betsey Nichols, 9 Sep 1810-5 Nov 1830.
SNOW, Joshua, Capt. - died 24 Apr 1839 at 79 yrs. 8 m. (Revolutionary War flag).
  Philena - wife of Abner B. Snow, died 14 May 1859 at 34 yrs. 9 m.
  Abner B. - died 3 Feb 1870 at 48 yrs.
  Estelle - dau of Abner B. & Philena Snow, died 22 Jan 1864 at 7 yrs. 9 m.
  Moses - father, died 26 Apr 1884 at 89 yrs. 7 m.

Deborah - mother, wife of Moses Snow, died 18 Oct 1874 at 80 yrs.

POTTER, Henry - died 5 Jun 1835 at 36 yrs. 8 m.
  Charles - son of Henry & Thankful Potter, died 6 Oct 1842 at 18 yrs. 8 m.
  Hannah J. - dau of Henry & Thankful Potter, died 23 Jul 1858 at 24 yrs. 9 m.
  Henry - son of Henry & Thankful Potter, died 17 Apr 1839 at 3 yrs. 4 m.
  Phebe - dau of Henry & Thankful Potter, died 1 Jul 1841 at 9 yrs. 9 m.

COOMBS, James - died 21 Sep 1880 at 81 yrs. 10 m.

BIBBER, Mary - mother, wife of Eri Bibber, died 17 Jul 1886 at 71 yrs. 5 m.
  Johnnie - (small broken stone).
  Charles Wilson, Dr. - 23 Apr 1876-29 Jul 1919.
  H. Abbie Adams - mother, his wife, died 1 Jun 1906 at 58 yrs. 1 m. 10 d.
  Benj. P. - father, died 19 Aug 1915 at 72 yrs. 4 m. Co. A 11 Regt. ME Vol. War 1861-65.

WEBBER, Dexter - died in Providence, RI, 28 Jun 1845 at 23 yrs.
  John - died 18 Nov 1845 at 21 yrs.
  Andrew - died 3 Sep 1849 at 18 yrs.
  Abby F. - died 6 Sep 1849 at 23 yrs.
  Mary H. - dau of David B. & Hannah Webber, died 8 Mar 1854 at 7 m. 8 d.

DOYLE, James - 1805-1864.
  Elizabeth L. - his wife, 1815-1888.
  Johnson J. - 1844-1910.
  J. Holman - 1846-1852.
  Jennie P. - 1851-1901.
  Georgia A. - 1859-1870.
  Chas. H. - 1846-1918.
  Priscilla J. - 1851-1901.

LINCOLN, Fred M. - only son of Elbridge & Eliza Lincoln, died 10 Oct 1873 at 22 yrs. 2 m.

STAPLES, Daniel - died 9 Feb 1832 at 55 yrs.

Rhoda - his wife, died 17 May 1855 at 78 yrs. 8 m.
Priscilla - dau of Alden & Eliza Staples, died 9 May 1844 at 13 m.
COOMBS, Joshua - died 29 Nov 1851 at 76 yrs.
Mary, Mrs. - wife of Joshua Coombs, died 18 Oct 1843 at 71 yrs.
Susan F. - dau of James & Love Coombs, died 3 Jan 1842 at 2 yrs. 6 m.
Love - wife of James Coombs, died 20 Dec 1851 at 50 yrs.
NOWELL, Milbury - died 29 Dec 1894 at 66 yrs. 2 m. 21 d.
Lizzie R. - wife of Milbury Nowell, died 13 Dec 1883 at 41 yrs. 4 m. 21 d.
Marianna P. - wife of Milbury Nowell, died 30 Jan 1913 at 74 yrs.
GUPTILL, Florence - 1866-1938 (on Nowell lot).
CAMPBELL, Mary E. - wife of Geo. D., died 11 Jun 1880 at 37 yrs.
Bertie - son of Geo. D. & Mary E. Campbell, died 29 Mar 1874 at 9 m.
Inf. dau of G. D. and M. E. Campbell, died 8 Jan 1866 at 3 wks.
WEBBER, Joseph - 1815-1895.
Susan - wife of Joseph Webber, 1813-1885.
CARD, Holmes A. - former husband of Susan Webber, lost at sea 26 Oct 1836 at 26 yrs.
George L. - 1834-   .)Children of
Susan E. - 1837-   .)Holmes A. and
Lydia A. - 1835-1853.)Susan Card
WEBBER, Viola S. - dau of J. D. and M. Webber, died 5 May 1884 at 9 yrs. 4 m.
Ida Estella - dau of J. H. and T. J. Webber, died 13 Nov 1874 at 3 yrs. 5 m.
Ezra C. - 29 Mar 1895-4 Jan 1952. PFC 104 Field Sig. Bn. Massachusetts, World War I.
Elisha S. - father, 1853-1934.

Alice A. - his wife, 1858-1942.
SYLVESTER, Samuel - 16 Oct 1844-23 Feb 1926.
  Ellen M. - wife of S. Sylvester, 25 Nov 1848-
  14 Jun 1892.
YEATON, Elizabeth - dau of A. and E. S. Yeaton,
  2 Sep 1905-2 Mar 1906 (on Sylvester stone).
SHAW, Thomas - 1832-1914.
  Jerusha A. - wife of T. Shaw, 1838-1908.
  Frank S. - son of T. and J. A. Shaw, 1866-
  1893.
  Benjamin - 1809-1894.
PLUMMER, Pennell - father, 18 Dec 1815-5 Mar
  1902.
  Hannah C. - wife of Pennell Plummer, 11 Nov
  1819-30 Sep 1898.
  Emeline P. - dau of Pennell & Hannah Plummer,
  died 24 Oct 1865 at 15 yrs. 2 m.
BENSON, Charles W. - 1854-1925.
  Elva M. - 1854-1902.
MERRYMAN, Benjamin - died 13 Feb 1865 at 74 yrs.
  Margaret - wife of Benjamin Merriman, died 17
  Aug 1853 at 57 yrs. 3 m.
PRESTON, Chas. - Co. F 24 ME Inf. (no dates).
COOMBS, Daniel C. - died 26 Sep 1891 at 63 yrs.
  6 m. 22 d.
  Emily - wife of Daniel C. Coombs, died 27 Jan
  1881 at 52 yrs. 10 m.
  Julia Ann - dau of Daniel C. & Emily Coombs,
  died 30 Dec 1863 at 4 yrs. 9 m.
  Elmer E. - son of Daniel C. & Emily Coombs,
  died 6 Aug 1864 at 9 m. 19 d.
  Elmer E. - son of Daniel C. & Emeline Coombs,
  died 17 Nov 1885 at 20 yrs. 6 m.
ROSS, Actor - 1820-1865, Co. B 15th ME Regt.
  Mabel W. - his wife, 1819-1913.
  Edward H. - died 10 Feb 1844 at 2 m. 15 d.
  Edward H. - died 25 Aug 1853 at 8 yrs. 7 m.
  Sons of Actor & Mabel W. Ross.

Charlotte E. - died 8 Sep 1857 at 4 yrs. 9 m.
Celestia M. - died 17 Dec 1924 at 73 yrs. 2 m.
CARTER, Daniel - died 14 Sep 1856 at 69 yrs. 10 m.
Harriet - wife of Daniel Carter, died 24 Aug 1883 at 92 yrs. 15 d.
Daniel, Jr. - died 22 Jun 1869 at 46 yrs.
DENNISON, Sarah A. - wife of A. K. Dennison, died 30 Dec 1857 at 25 yrs. 11 m. (on Carter lot).
EMERSON, D. F. - 5 Oct 1858-19 Apr 1912 ("Fred" on top of stone).
Mary P. Carter - wife of William J. Emerson, 8 Apr 1834-14 Mar 1903.
William J. - 4 Sep 1837-25 Jun 1898 (Civil War marker).
DEYMORE, Amanda - wife of Henry Deymore, died 24 Dec 1860 at 30 yrs. 4 m. (baby bur with mother).
SENIOR, Josephine A. - only child of Joseph & Melinda Senior, died 20 Apr 1858 at 4 yrs. 11 m.
AVERY, Isaiah A. - 1853-1898.
Adelaide E. - his wife, 1856-1914.
Harry A. - 1884-1884.)
Ida M. - 1885-1916.   ) Their
Arthur D. - 1887-1926.) Children
Inez M. - 1883-1942.)
Oscar O. - 1889-1929.)
BENNETT, Abby V. - died 14 Oct 1857 at 2 yrs. 7 m. 9 d.
Mary L. - died 24 Sep 1857 at 5 m. 1 d.
Children of Francis & Mary Bennett
Abbie V. - dau of Francis & Mary Bennett, died 16 Apr 1860 at 9 m.
CARR, Lemont P. - 28 Sep 1819-25 Dec 1874.
Miranda T. - his wife, 23 Sep 1829-23 Apr 1901.

Hix Small Cemetery - at the intersection of Routes 201 and 125, take Route 125 towards Bowdoin Center. Take first right turn on to Lewis Hill Road. Go 1.9 miles and turn left. After turning, go short distance, and you will see signs for the cemetery.

WILSON, Maria A. - wife of Albert M. Wilson, died 29 Apr 1890 at 27 yrs. 5 m.
  Bertie E. - son of A. M. & M. A. Wilson, died 8 Sep 1883 at 11 m. 22 d.
MITCHELL, Hiram S., Eld. - 1833-1903.
  Elizabeth - wife of Hiram S. Mitchell, 1836-1925.
  (one field stone)
SMALL, Marion - 1909-1909.
  Frank E. - 1872-1945.
  Harriet T. - his wife, 1879-1918.
  Stanley M. - Maine Sgt. Co. M 103 Inf. World War II BSM-PH, 7 Oct 1915-19 Jul 1969.
SAUNDERS, Amy E. - wife of Jessie T. Saunders, 1887-1938.
FREEMAN, Alonzo H. - 1906-1964.
SHEEN, Raymond Anson - Maine PFC Co. C 34 Inf. World War II, 10 Nov 1922-13 Jul 1972.
SMITH, Harry L., III - 24 Oct 1966-27 Jan 1967.
HATCH, Joseph R. - 1860-1916.
  Flora E. - his wife, 1861-1926.
WEST, Perl O. - 1876-1955.
  Clairibel B. - 1883-   .
BUKER, Eugene T. - 17 Dec 1850-9 Feb 1921.
  Lucy M. Chuck - his wife, 29 Apr 1861-19 Mar 1951.
  Olivia D. - mother, wife of Wm. G. Buker, Jr., 31 Dec 1836-30 Jun 1909.
  Wm. G., Jr. - father, Co. B 15th ME Vols., 14 Feb 1834-3 Jul 1912 (GAR marker & flag).
  E. V. L. - 1906-1931 (on Buker lot).

REID, Elmer Douglas - 1926-1926 (funeral home marker).
John S. - 1905- .
Winnifred M. - his wife, 1908- .
LEWIS, Daisy - dau of Jacob W. & Clara C. Lewis, died 8 Sep 1890 at 1 yr. 4 m.
Geo. W. - 6 Oct 1875-22 Jul 1895.
ALLEN, Elijah, Jr. - Corp'l. Co. E (GAR stand & flag) - stone sunk so dates cannot be read).
BUKER, David A. - son of Wm. G. and Caroline Buker, died 6 May 1936 at 7 wks.
(Field stone next to David A.)
Bethia, Mrs. - wife of Dea. David Buker, died 9 Nov 1834 at 70 yrs.
David, Dea. - died 12 May 1838 at 77 yrs.
SMALL, Joseph, Mr. - died 13 Feb 1831 at 83 yrs. (Per DAR Application #527809, b. 24 Aug 1748).
Mindy, Mrs. - died 15 Mar 1833 at 85 yrs.
Taylor, Mr. - died 17 Dec 1829 at 83 yrs.
Mary, Mrs. - widow of Mr. Taylor Small, died 19 Dec 1836 at 88 yrs.
MINOTT, Jennie W. - dau of George & Lavina Minott, died 6 Mar 1879 at 9 yrs. 6 m. (Another stone gives yr. of b. as 1869.)
Lavina - wife of George Minott, died 17 Mar 1879 at 32 yrs. 6 m.
Geo. - 1846-1914.
His wives -
Lavina - 1846-1879.
Charity -1848-1909 (a head stone gives C.A.M.).
Nellie R. - 1875-1937.
Mary Sampson - born 25 Jan 1832, died 24 Mar 1909.
Sarah - mother, wife of Charles Minott, died 8 Nov 1889 at 85 yrs.
Charles - father, died 6 Nov 1876 at 75 yrs. 3 m.
SMALL, Elisha - died 22 Feb 1879 at 56 yrs.

Martha E. - wife of Elisha Small, 1828-1888.
Jesse - 1815-1907.
Marcia - wife of Jessie Small, died 3 Apr 1891 at 71 yrs.
Hannah - died 15 Aug 1831 at 23 yrs.
Ruth - wife of Taylor Small, died 6 Sep 1867 at 86 yrs. 6 m.
Taylor - died 4 May 1829 at 51 yrs.
DOYLE, Laura E. - wife of Llewellyn P. Doyle, died 2 Jul 1867 at 20 yrs.
Llewellyn P. - died 22 Dec 1870 at 33 yrs.
BUKER, William G. - died 25 Jul 1869 at 65 yrs. 7 d.
Caroline W. - wife of William G. Buker, died 28 May 1897 at 91 yrs. 8 m.
Irene A. - dau of Wm. G. & Caroline Buker, died 21 Dec 1851 at 20 yrs.
Martha Ann - dau of William G. & Caroline Buker, died 22 Feb 1858 at 18 yrs.
RIDLEY, Eliza J. - departed this life 2 Jul 1870 at 55 yrs. 2 m. 21 d. (wife of Ruben Ridley - epitaph refers to "Mother").
BRIMIJON, Nancy A. - died 30 Aug 1873 at 20 yrs. 7 m.
Lizzie H. - died 25 Jul 1890 at 40 yrs.
LEWIS, Eleanor C. - mother (wife of John A. Lewis), died 13 Jun 1897 at 86 yrs. 10 m. 26 d.
John A. - died 25 Feb 1892 at 87 yrs. 4 m. 29 d.
COLE, Llewellyn E.)iron plaque on
  Addie F.)field stone
  Isaac)with no
HUNT, Sophia A.)dates
VARNEY, Hicks S. - born 30 Oct 1818, died 26 Sep 1901.
Adaline - wife of Hicks S. Varney, born 28 Aug 1820, died 18 Sep 1892.
Alonzo N. - at 4 yrs. 4 m. (no dates).

Martha C. - at 3 yrs. 5 m. (no dates).
Children of Hicks S. & Adaline Varney
SMALL, Scott - 23 Mar 1880-10 Feb 1943.
  Cornelius C. - father, 1852-1938.
  Marietta Hogan - his wife, 1853-1928.
  Taylor - son of George & Lois Small, died 22 Aug 1852.
  Louis - mother, wife of George Small, died 1 Jan 1878 at 69 yrs. 5 m.
  George - father, died 17 Sep 1894 at 89 yrs. 3 m.
  Margaret L. - dau of George & Lois Small, died 14 Sep 1848 at 3 yrs. 8 m.
  Taylor - died 4 May 1829 at 51 yrs.
CAMPBELL, Abigail, Mrs. - wife of Daniel Campbell, died 25 Oct 1847 at 75 yrs. 7 m.
  Daniel - died 21 Aug 1856 at 83 yrs. 10 m.
CHANDLER, Charles C. - son of Wm. P. & Dorcas H. Chandler, died 21 Oct 1865 at 22 yrs. 10 m.
  Dorcas H. - wife of Wm. P. Chandler, died 22 Nov 1899 at 82 yrs. 2 m.
  William P. - died 10 May 1886 at 72 yrs. 3 m.
CHASE, Caroline K. - wife of Albion Chase, died 3 Apr 1858 at 24 yrs. 1 m.
  (There are three field stones on this lot.)
SMALL, Mary - wife of Hix Small, died 12 Sep 1852 at 86 yrs.
  Hix, Mr. - died 20 May 1826 at 60 yrs.
  (There is a field stone on this lot.)
  Zaccheus - father, died 30 Sep 1884 at 79 yrs.
  Rozilla - mother, wife of Zaccheus Small, died 20 May 1896 at 85 yrs. 10 m.
  Alonzo - son of Zaccheus & Rozilla Small, died 7 Jul 1854 at 20 yrs. 5 m.
  Hannah - dau of Zaccheus & R. Small, died 6 Sep 1844 at 2 yrs. 5 m.
  Caroline - dau of Abizer & Ruth Small, died 8 Jan 1861 at 31 yrs.

Ruth - wife of Abizer Small, died 12 Jan 1841 at 48 yrs.
Abizer - died 28 Sep 1839 at 44 yrs. 3 (?) m. (There are two field stones on this lot.)
Dianna - 9 Nov 1824-23 Mar 1910.
Judah B. - 30 Dec 1820-13 Apr 1903.
Abiezer - died 2 Dec 1900 at 68 yrs. 4 m. 12 d.

SMITH, Mehitable - wife of Geor. W. (?) Smith, died 3 Mar 1893 at 74 yrs. (on lot with Judah B. Small).

SMALL, Charles C. - died 24 May 1874 at 38 yrs. 8 m.

FREEMAN, Vesta S. - sister, died 25 Jan 1937 at 58 yrs.
Robert G. - brother, died 19 May 1896 at 29 yrs.
James C. - father, died 30 Oct 1879 at 40 yrs.
Ellen F. - wife of James C., died 23 Oct 1924 at 82 yrs.

CHANDLER, Alonzo S. - son of Geo. & Nancie J. Chandler, died 14 May 1861 at 2 m.

CAMPBELL, Martha J. - dau of C. & A. Campbell, died 7 Sep 1853 at 2 yrs. 6 m.
(Field stone with what appears to be "B.J.D. 1841" and field stone marked "E.D.C.).
Geo. - died 30 Sep 1863 at 67 yrs. 10 m. 10 d.
Martha - wife of Geo. Campbell, died 20 Jan 1855 at 57 yrs.
Charles H. - son of Hiram & Mary B. Campbell, died 29 Oct 1863 at 4 yrs. 8 m.
George E. - son of Eld. Hiram & Mary B. Campbell, drowned 2 Jul 1875 at 22 yrs 5 m.

SMALL, Hix - 1796-1864.
Rachel Ridley - mother, his wife, 1796-1851.
Daniel R. - 1825-1879   )Their
LAPHAM, Mary Esther - 1839-   . Children

SMALL, Hicks - 1828-1905.
  Mary Brown - his wife, 1830-1858.
CARD, Lydia Ann - died 2 Nov 1853 at 18 yrs.
ENNIS, Hannah - died 30 Nov 1882 at 60 yrs. 7 m.
SMALL, Rachel - wife of Thomas Small, died 14 Dec 1859 at 69 yrs. 8 m.
  Artemas F. - son of Elisha & Ruth Small, died 17 May 1851 at 2 yrs. 6 m.
  Polly - wife of Jonathan Small, died 30 Sep 1872 at 81 yrs.
BOOKER, J. - 1828-1911.
  Rebecca H. - his wife, died 11 Dec 1864 at 33 yrs.
  Mary L. - his 2nd wife, died 4 Sep 1887 at 40 yrs. 11 m.
  Georgiana - died 2 Dec 1864 at 5 yrs. 9 m.
  Baby - died 15 Dec 1864 at 10 m.
  Children of J. & Rebecca H. Booker
  Martha V. - 1856-1941.
JASPER, Maurice - 1901-1918 (on Booker stone).
DOYLE, Elisha - 25 Feb 1830-6 Jun 1911.
  Mary H. - his wife, 11 Jul 1850-10 Feb 1928.
SMALL, Albra J. - (no dates).
  Lizzie E. - his wife, (no dates).
  Ralph - aged 2 m. (no dates).
  Rosilla A. - wife of Joseph G. Small, 30 Mar 1844-4 Sep 1926.
  Joseph G. - 11 Aug 1840-8 Nov 1904.
  M. Cecile - 1884-1958.
GROVER, Viola V. - 1852-1932.
  George T. - 1839-1926.
TEMPLE, John - died 1 Aug 1844 at 43 yrs.
  Mindwell - wife of William W. Temple, died 27 Aug 1856 at 80 yrs.
  Wm. W. - died 21 Feb 1859 at 80 yrs.
WEBBER, Lula L. - dau of J. H. and Frances Webber, died 17 Sep 1863 at 5 yrs. 10 m. 21 d.

James H. - 1831-1900.
Frances A. - his wife, 1832-1906.
CAMPBELL, Zilpha - wife of Chas. Campbell, died 10 Nov 1857 at 50 yrs. 9 m.
Charles - 1806-1885.
Eunice G. - his wife, 1820-1916.
Wm. - died 14 Apr 1876 at 79 yrs.
Lydia - his wife, died 22 Apr 1833 at 37 yrs.
Lettice - his wife, died 7 Apr 1876 at 84 yrs.
Albion H. - 1 Dec 1823-3 Apr 1897, Co. C 6th ME Regt.
DOYLE, Adaline - wife of Michael Doyle, died 7 Nov 1873 at 65 yrs. 8 m.
BICKFORD, Jonathan L. - died 27 Aug 1860 at 41 yrs.
Ruth - wife, died 9 Oct 1884 at 64 yrs.
Their sons
John L. - Killed the Battle of the Wilderness 6 May 1864 at 21 yrs.
George - died 14 Nov 1850 at 3 yrs.
BUKER, Isaac B., Dea. - died 18 Nov 1885 at 87 yrs.
His wives
Roxanna - died 9 Jan 1852 at 51 yrs.
Mehitable - died 26 Aug 1871 at 67 yrs.
Wm. G. - died 13 Aug 1829 at 2 yrs. 7 m.
Henry S. - died 1845 at 24 yrs.
Harriet - died 19 Aug 1869 at 30 yrs. 6 m.
Children of Isaac & Roxanna Buker
SMALL, Artemas G. - 1824-1861.
EATON, Catherine A. - wife of Nathan Eaton - formerly wife of Artemas G. Small, 1830-1919 (bur with Artemas Small).
THOMPSON, William - born 30 May 1759, died Nov 1815.
Mary - his wife, born 1744, died Feb 1814.
BUKER, Samuel - died 29 Jun 1875 at 84 yrs. 8 m. (stone broken).

Sally – our mother, wife of Samuel Buker, died 12 Apr 1872 at 79 yrs. 1 m. 3 d.
BICKFORD, John – died 15 Jun 1862 at 77 yrs. 3 m.
  Sophia – wife of John Bickford, died 20 Feb 1883 at 92 yrs. 9 m.

  The pains of death are past
  Labor and sorrow cease
  And life's long warfare, closed at last
  Her soul is found in peace

ALEXANDER, Mustard – died 23 Apr 1869 at 63 yrs. 6 m.
  Lydia – wife of Mustard, died 8 Feb 1896 at 89 yrs. 3 m. 30 d.
SMALL, Hicks – 1828-1905.
  Mary E. – his wife, 1830-1858.
COOMBS, Mary A. – dau of Abner & Mary A. Coombs, died 4 Jul 1864 at 21 d.
  Dennie – (no dates).
  Harriet – wife of Abner Coombs, died 8 Jul 1855 at 40 yrs. 6 m.
  Abner – died 28 May 1873 at 65 yrs. 9 m.
  Mary Ann – wife of Abner Coombs, born 11 Oct 1825, died 22 Mar 1905.
  (Stone for Abner & Mary Ann "Erected by Their Son Bert D. Coombs 1934.")
  Roy H. – born 3 Jul 1883, died 25 Jan 1899, "Only son of E. S. and V. S. Coombs."
BICKFORD, Silas A. – 1859-1941.
  Matilda A. – 1864-1941.

West Bowdoin Cemetery - at the junction of Route 196 and Route 125 in Lisbon Falls, take Route 125 (Main St.) towards Bowdoin. Go 4 1/10th miles. Turn left on Store Road. At the first four corners, turn right and drive 3/10th of a mile. The cemetery is on the left adjacent to the West Bowdoin Baptist Church. However, they are not affiliated. These inscriptions were copied in 1991 and 1992.

SMALL, Stephen - 1825-1906.
  Lucy - 1827-1913.
  William F. - 1857-   .
  Laura E. - dau of Stephen & Lucy Small, died 21 Mar 1860 at 7 m. 11 d.
  Inf. - died 14 Aug 1849 (no stone, but in cem. records).
  Charles - son of Joshua & Cynthia Small, died 7 Apr 1860 at 11 m. 6 d.
NOYES, Laura E. - 1861-1884 (on Small lot).
MAXWELL, John - died 17 Aug 1883 at 69 yrs.
  Eliza A. - his wife, died 19 Aug 1903 at 86 yrs.
  Abby - died 16 Apr 1855 at 35 yrs.
  Geo. - died 15 Nov 1860 at 36 yrs.
  Thomas - died 16 Oct 1857 at 85 yrs.
  Martha - his wife, died 9 Oct 1857 at 57 yrs.
PURINGTON, Washington - died 18 Sep 1868 at 68 yrs.
  Sally C. - wife of Washington Purington, died 18 Sep 1884 at 80 yrs.
  Mary J. - dau of Washington & Sally Purington, died 17 Nov 1834 at 2 yrs.
  (Small stone - not readable.)
THOMPSON, Frances Nowell - 1857-1934 (Bowdoin Town Report for Year Ending 10 Feb 1935 states Francis D. Thompson died 3 Jul 1934 at 76 yrs. 9 m. 2 d).

Ethel M. - 1880-1897.
Guy M. - 1886-1931. Children
NOWELL, Delia G. - 1832-1857 (on Thompson stone).
BUBIER, Rachel - wife of John, died 30 Jul 1865 at 67 yrs. 8 m. 11 d.

Ye living men as you pass by,
As you are now so once was I,
As I am now, soon you must be
Prepare for death, and follow me.

William - died 28 Aug 1875 at 56 yrs. 8 m. 28 d.
Philenia W. - wife of William Bubier, died 6 Dec 1865 at 38 yrs. 3 m. 15 d.
CURTIS, Lester G. - 4 Jun 1880-3 Aug 1951.
BUBIER, Emily C. - dau of William & Philenia W. Bubier, died 31 Jul 1862 at 7 yrs. 9 m. 12 d.
Mark - War of 1812 (cemetery records do not show anyone bur. here, but Town Selectmen's records show Mark Bubier).
BOOBIER, Daniel - Co. A 12 ME Inf. (GAR marker) (no dates).
JOHNSON, Wm. E. - died 22 Jun 1909 at 64 yrs. 7 m.
Dora - wife of William E. Johnson, died 24 Aug 1882 at 28 yrs. 5 m.
Wm. E. - died 15 Sep 1909 at 38 yrs. 11 m.
DUNN, William - Medal of Honor QM, U. S. Navy, 28 Apr 1834-18 Mar 1902 (letter from Medal of Honor Historical Society states: "Medal of Honor for action on board U.S.S. Monadnock during the attack on Fort Fisher, NC 24-25 Dec 1864 during the Civil War").
Susan T. - mother, 1837-1917.
John H. - 1859-1938.
William F. - 1866-1945.
Minnie B. - 1873-1880.

GOWELL, Franklin W. - 1852-1926.
  Jennie A. - his wife, 1859-1943.
  Mabel B. - 1876-1878.
  Cora M. - 1886-1970. Children
CANHAM, Elizabeth G. (nee Gowell) (NSDAR marker),
  1879-1952.
  Vincent W. - 1876-1942.
GILPATRICK, Mary W. - wife of Nathaniel Gilpatrick, died 4 Mar 1870 at 82 yrs. 1 m. 20 d.
  Nathaniel - died 23 Jun 1866 at 80 yrs. 13 d.
PLUMMER, William F. - son of Wm. G. & Susan D. Plummer, died 6 Feb 1854 at 1 y. 4 m.
SALLEY, Wm. H. - died 29 Jul 1882 at 55 yrs.
  Mary A. - his wife, died 10 Dec 1883 at 49 yrs.
  Bertie F. - son of W. H. & Mary A. Salley, died 28 Mar 1867 at 17 m.
  Trying Gilbert - son of G. H. & Ida A. M. Salley, died 16 Jan 1900 at 9 m. 20 d.
BOOKER, James B. - died 4 Dec 1854 at 21 yrs.
  William W. - died 13 Aug 1861 at 22 yrs.
  Sons of Isaac R. and Hannah Booker.
  Isaac R. - died 27 May 1868 at 60 yrs.
  Hannah - his wife, died 2 Jun 1867 at 55 yrs.
  Irving G. - (head stone only; dates not readable).
  (Bookers are on same stone as Salley family.)
MARR, Winter - died 15 Dec 1889 at 76 yrs.
  Jane - died 2 Jan 1897 at 84 yrs.
  Arrobine - 1845-1847.
  Marshall R. - 1850-1853.
  Arrobine - 1856-1857.
  Sidney - Co. C 6th Mich Cav. 1837-1864, died at Richmond, VA.
PURINTON, Jos. C., Dea. - died 18 Dec 1882 at 64 yrs.
  Octavia - his wife, died 25 Jun 1903 at 80 yrs.

Nath'l, Rev. - died 12 Jun 1862 at 74 yrs.
Priscilla - his wife, died 14 Aug 1860 at 72 yrs.
Mary Ann - their dau, died 22 Sep 1868 at 41 yrs.
Samuel - died 5 Dec 1836 at 20 yrs.
Hannah - died 11 Dec 1838 at 18 yrs.
Children of N. & P. Purinton.
Clara - died 29 Apr 1924 at 71 yrs.
Israel - (head stone with both names
Nancy -   but no dates).
Albert W., Rev. - died 10 May 1878 at 66 yrs. 10 m.
Sally - wife, died 22 Jan 1866 at 53 yrs. 9 m.
Rebecca E. - died 20 Feb 1866 at 18 yrs.
Lucinda J. - died 22 Sep 1839 at 10 m.
Children of Rev. A. W. and S. R. Purinton.
Willie - son of N. S. and J. E. Purinton, died 6 Oct 1867 at 5 wks.
COX, Alfred, Dea. - father, died 30 Mar 1877 at 64 yrs. 11 m.
Sarah A. - wife of Alfred Cox, 12 Nov 1823- 17 Nov 1914.
Edgar W. - son of Alfred and Mariam Cox, died 18 Apr 1866 at 16 yrs.
Miriam - wife of Alfred Cox, died 28 Apr 1860 at 54 yrs. 2 m.
Hannah A. - dau of Alfred & Miriam Cox, died 15 Sep 1841 at 11 m.
Melville A. - son of Alfred & Miriam Cox, died 22 Aug 1848 (age may be under ground).
Solon E. - son of Alfred & Miriam Cox, died 4 Sep 1848 at 1 yr.
REED, Elizabeth S. - wife of Marshall Reed, died 6 Oct 1855 at 29 yrs.
PARKER, Joseph - died 10 May 1849 at 74 yrs.
THOMPSON, Cornelius - died 15 Nov 1857 at 66 yrs. 7 m.

Sarah — wife of Cornelius Thompson, died 8 Dec 1830 at 34 yrs.
Caroline M. — dau of Cornelius & Sarah Thompson, died 3 Oct 1840 at 21 yrs.
Henry H. — son of Cornelius & Sarah Thompson, born 1 Nov 1821, died 20 Feb 1874 at 52 yrs. 3 m. 20 d.
Abigail S. — wife of Cornelius Thompson, died 11 Apr 1885 at 89 yrs. 11 m. 7 d.

COX, Martha T. — wife of Cyrus B. Cox, died 22 Mar 1912 at 76 yrs. 8 m. 17 d.
Cyrus B. — husband, died 22 Apr 1876 at 60 yrs. 11 m.

PARKER, Alfred B. — died 2 Apr 1858 at 21 yrs. 10 m.
Charles W. — son of Israel W. & Paulena Parker, died 15 Dec 1873 at 20 yrs. 3 m.
Lizzie S. — dau of Israel W. & Paulena Parker, died 8 Oct 1863 at 5 yrs. 10 m.
Israel W. — 1811-1857.
Paulena Eaton — his wife, 1817-1903.
Winfield S. — 1847-1848.) Children of
Eugene H. — 1849-1893.) I. W. and
Charles W. — 1853-1874.) P. E.
Sarah E. — 1858-1863.) Parker

GOULD, Edmund — 1812-1891.
Eliza — wife of Edmund Gould, 1811-1870.
J. Mellen — son of Edmund & Eliza Gould, died 1 Feb 1864 at 25 yrs. 7 m. 20 d.
George N. O. — son of Edmund & Eliza Gould, died 30 Sep 1853 at 10 m. 7 d.
Lydia Jane — dau of Edmund & Eliza Gould, died 10 Jun 1859 at 18 yrs. 9 m.

RANDALL, Harriet A. — 1845-1926.

JOHNSON, Martha E. — dau of John & Martha Johnson, died 22 Feb 1861 at 10 m.
John F. — son of John & Martha Johnson, died 21 Oct 1873 at 20 yrs. 6 m. 18 d.

God takes the beautiful, the best
They are but lent, not given.
He sets his jewels on his breast.
That they may shine in heaven.

   Martha - mother, 1817-1893.
   John - father, 1816-1888.
HIGGINS, Zacheus B. - died 24 Aug 1879 at 79 yrs. 5 m.
   Mary L. - wife of Zacheus B. Higgins, died 23 Jul 1853 at 58 yrs. 8 m.
   Nancy W. - wife of Zacheus Higgins, died 8 Nov 1899 at 81 yrs. 3 m.
   Fannie E. - wife of Martin V. Higgins, died 5 May 1883 at 23 yrs.
   Martin V. B. - died 11 May 1901 at 63 yrs. 4 m.
WILLIAMS, Clarence E. - 1854-1902.
   Martha J. - his wife, 1854-1923.
   Edith V. - 1879-1896.
   Infant - 1891-1891.
   John - 1803-1876.
   Catherine - his wife, 1803-1851.
   Judith D. -his wife, 1822-1900.
WOODARD, Roscoe D. - died 23 Jun 1876 at 28 yrs. 2 m.
   Charles B. - son of A. F. and Hannah Woodard, died 2 Apr 1883 at 37 yrs. 3 m.
COOMBS, Nat'l G. - 5 Feb 1821-20 Oct 1876.
   Rachel - wife, 15 Jul 1823-16 Oct 1902.
ALLEN, Della - born 6 Mar 1861, died 15 Oct 1878 ("Allen" not on stone, but Della was an Allen per cemetery records).
   Hannah S. Coombs - wife of William C. Allen. 6 Apr 1843-2 Mar 1911.
   William C. - died 22 Sep 1875 at 37 yrs. 8 m. (There is a GAR marker for William.)
BOWIE, Anna L. - mother, wife of Rev. R. S. Bowie, died 7 Sep 1886 at 86 yrs.

MUDGE, Chas. R., Lt. Col. - Camp N21 (no stone; cemetery records show "Lynn, Mass. Camp" - no dates; bur. on Horatio Small lot).
SMALL, Horatio G. - 16 Jul 1833-6 Apr 1888. Corp. Co. E. 23, ME Vols., Private Co. A29 ME Vols.
  Lizzie E. - wife, 1845-1910.
  Frederick H. - son, 1869-1900.
GARLAND, William E. - 18 Jan 1860-21 Oct 1932.
  Hannah Hall - 3 Nov 1864-16 Mar 1951.
  Grace May - 10 May 1898-6 Aug 1921.
  Ralston A. - 23 Nov 1894-15 May 1908.
PURINTON, Lila Garland - 24 Aug 1887-10 Nov 1980.
TARR, Rebecca M. - wife of Alonzo L. Tarr, died 10 Feb 1890 at 48 yrs. 3 m. 13 d.
  Alonzo L. - 1843-1917.
  Chester L. - 1879-1917.
HALL, David Purinton - 7 Oct 1942-
  Ruth Purinton - 19 Dec 1914-
  Marchant Hodsdon - 27 Feb 1915
GARDNER, Rebecca Purinton Hall - 5 Nov 1945- (David Hall through Rebecca Gardner on Garland lot.)
CAMPBELL, Adelia E. - mother, wife of John B. Campbell, died 28 Dec 1883 at 26 yrs. 1 m.
SHEPHARD, Luke - father, 26 Mar 1824-4 Jul 1866.
  Mehitabel J. - mother, 29 Sep 1829-22 Feb 1902 (cemetery records show her maiden name was Grover).
  Rebecca - (no dates).
  Marjorie - (stone cannot be read, but cemetery records show Marjorie died 1871).
  Marsailes - (per cemetery records - no dates).
SMITH, David - 1825-1909.
  Amanda Bradley - his wife, 1827-1922.
  Charles B. - 1867-1926.
  Susan A. - 1858-1875.
  Jeanie Marr - 1864-1925.

William A. - 1861-1881.
GETCHELL, Bethiah H. - wife of David C. Getchell, died 29 Jul 1866 at 50 yrs. 1 m. 19 d.
COOMBS, Josephine Chase - wife of W. A. Coombs, 1862-1929.
  Lizzie Emily - dau of William A. & Lavina Coombs, died 8 Sep 1865 at 6 m. 20 d.
WILLIAMS, Lewellyn - 3 Dec 1828-6 May 1900.
  Melinda - his wife, 6 Dec 1834-1 Feb 1933.
  Alphonso - their son, 6 May 1856-20 Jun 1906.
SHEPPHARD, George E. - 1863-1912.
  Ada Johnson - his wife, 18__-1888.
  Eva M. - 1892-1977.
  Herbert E. - 1897-1969.
WEBBER, Enoch L. - died 25 May 1891 at 60 yrs.
  Mahala G. - wife of Enoch L. Webber, died 21 May 1922 at 84 yrs. 10 m.
SMALL, Huldah - wife of Wm. Small, died 11 Apr 1864 at 58 yrs. 6 m.
  William - died 18 Jan 1891 at 88 yrs.
DENHAM, James - died 15 Mar 1864 at 69 yrs. 9 m.
  Louisa - wife of James Denham, died 21 Nov 1869 at 69 yrs. 9 m.
COOMBS, Agnes R. - wife of Robert Coombs & dau of J. and L. Denham, died 17 Jul 1853 at 19 yrs. 17 d.
DENHAM, James Herbert, II - 1868-1962.
  Cora M. - his wife, 1868-1953.
  James P. - 1831-1909.
  Huldah Small - his wife, 1835-1929.
  James Herbert - their son, 1861-1963.
JONES, William W. - 1 May 1822-30 Jan 1904.
  His wives
  Sebrina R. - 24 May 1827-3 Apr 1857.
  Ella Coombs - 11 Oct 1829-18 Nov 1873.
  Dexter W. - died 30 Jun 1853 at 24 yrs. 8 m. 10 d.
  Elijah, Jr. - died 26 Mar 1867 at 73 yrs. 4 m.

Betsey - wife of Elijah Jones, Jr., died 3
　　Feb 1855 at 56 yrs. 7 m.
　　Fred H. - 7 May 1863-26 Oct 1873.
　　Fannie E. - 18 Jul 1868-15 Nov 1873.
　　Children of W. W. & E. C. Jones.
BENSON, Agnes D. - sister, 1858-1920.
　　Frank -　　　　)cemetery records show
　　Abbie Gowell -)these names for 3
　　George W. -　　)unmarked graves
　　Catharine Denham - mother, wife of George F.
　　Benson, died 18 Mar 1892 at 69 yrs. 1 m.
　　George F. - father, died 15 Jun 1863 at 49
　　yrs. 8 m.
YORK, Samuel T. - died 1 Jun 1886 at 69 yrs.
　　Anna J. - wife of Samuel T. York, died 16 Feb
　　1871 at 50 yrs. 8 m. 18 d.
　　Sarah L. - died 25 Oct 1873 at 17 yrs.
　　Mary E. - died 3 Apr 1874 at 21 yrs.
　　Daughters of Samuel T. & Anna J. York.
　　Olive A. - wife of Samuel T. York, died 16 Apr
　　1893 at 73 yrs. 2 m.
JENKINS, Rodney F. - brother, died 1 Sep 1895 at
　　69 yrs. (on York lot).
FISHER, Sewall - 23 May 1818-6 Aug 1894.
　　Abby Adams - his wife, 7 Sep 1836-21 Feb 1913.
　　Oscar S. - 25 Oct 1866-29 Mar 1883.
　　Frank P. - 20 Apr 1870-3 Sep 1895.
　　Scott W. - 9 Apr 1864-30 Jan 1922.
LESAN, Charles E. - 1908-1981 (on Springer lot).
　　Charles E., Jr. - 1943-1977 (on Springer
　　stone).
SPRINGER, Boyd O. - 1910-1984.
　　Winnifred E. - his wife, 1912-1987.
　　R. Franklin - 1913-1951 (child of Rufus and
　　Dorothy Springer).
　　Rufus F. - 1871-1941.
　　Dorothy L. - his wife, 1880-1952.
　　Douglas L. - Maine, CM3, U. S. Navy, World

War II, 27 May 1915-8 Apr 1952 (child of Rufus and Dorothy Springer).
GROVER, Tallman - died 17 Oct 1823 at 13 m.
  Tallman - died 20 Sep 1826 at 2 yrs. 1 m.
  Children of Jane & Thomas Grover.
  William K. - died 2 May 1831 at 10 yrs. 5 m.
  Infant - son died 26 Jul 1827.
  Children of Jane & Thomas Grover.
  Thomas - died 10 Jan 1858 at 64 yrs. 3 m.
BUBIER, Jane - wife of Otis Bubier, died 14 Jun 1869 at 72 yrs. (on Grover lot).
GILLESPIE, Thomas - died 15 Jan 1866 at 63 yrs. 3 m. 16 d.
  Catherine B. - wife of Thomas Gillespie, died 27 Jun 1894 at 83 yrs. 10 m.
  Julia A. - dau of Thomas & Catharine B. Gillespie, died 15 Jun 1864 at 25 yrs. 9 m. 11 d.
  Charles C. - brother, son of Thomas & Catharine B. Gillespie, died 3 Oct 1870 at 21 yrs. 3 m. 3 d.
  Tillie - died 1882 at 29 yrs.
  Thomas - died 16 Nov 1919 at 85 yrs. 7 m. 6 d.
  May F. - born 22 Oct 1856, died 5 Jan 1939.
  Henry - died 21 Jul 1923 at 45 yrs. 9 m.
BOOKER, Samuel - died 24 Apr 1859 at 21 yrs. 3 m. 8 d.
  Joseph W. - died 27 Jan 1860.
  David - died 4 Aug 1848 at 22 yrs.
HIGGINS, Andrew C. - husband, died 22 Oct 1882 at 32 yrs. 10 m.
BATCHELDER, Ella S. - wife of Samuel Batchelder, former wife of Andrew C. Higgins, 24 May 1852-3 Apr 1935.
HIGGINS, Jeremiah - died 16 May 1858 at 40 yrs.
  Phebe T. - his wife, died 29 Jan 1864 at 48 yrs.
  Philip - died 30 Nov 1836 at 21 yrs.

Rachel - wife of Capt. Jeremiah Higgins, died 20 Apr 1845 at 40 yrs. 9 m.
Jeremiah, Capt. - died 25 Jul 1867 at 81 yrs. 5 m.
COTTON, William S., Col. - died 13 Apr 1888 at 72 yrs. 9 m. 8 d. (GAR marker).
Mary M. - wife of Col. William S. Cotton, died 23 Mar 1872 at 52 yrs. 5 m.
Louisa D. - dau of Wm. S. & Mary M. Cotton, died 14 Feb 1859 at 13 yrs. 10 d.
Minerva J. - dau of William S. & Mary M. Cotton, died 29 Mar 1860 at 11 yrs. 11 m. 27 d.
M. Ella - dau of Wm. S. & Mary M. Cotton, died 8 Aug 1874 at 17 yrs. 1 m. 5 d.
TARR, Emily - dau of Daniel M. & Hannah Tarr, died 31 Dec 1874 at 20 yrs.
Daniel H. - son of Daniel M. & Hannah Tarr, died 26 Jun 1872 at 11 yrs. 1 m.
Abial L. - son of Daniel M. & Hannah Tarr, died 30 Sep 1872 at 20 yrs.
Cora B. - dau of Daniel M. & Hannah Tarr, died 25 Oct 1881 at 15 yrs. 11 m.
Hannah - wife of Daniel M. Tarr, died 10 Jun 1867 at 41 yrs. 1 m.
Daniel M. - died 30 Nov 1874 at 50 yrs. 9 m. 6 d. (GAR marker).
Hannah J. - dau of Paul & Hannah Tarr, died 12 Nov 1856 at 21 yrs. 7 m.
Hannah - wife of Paul Tarr, died 9 Nov 1864 at 64 yrs. 4 m. 14 d.
Paul - died 1 Feb 1861 at 65 yrs. 9 m. 3 d.
ALLEN, Elijah - died 23 Mar 1867 at 66 yrs. 3 m. 12 d.
Margaret - mother, wife of Elijah Allen, died 3 Apr 1880 at 79 yrs.
Lorany - dau of Elijah & Margaret Allen, died 6 Nov 1839 at 21 m.

RIDEOUT, Margaret A. Allen - wife of Andrew J.
  Rideout, 1829-1880.
  Geo. F. - papa, 16 Jul 1852-23 Apr 1913.
ARNO, Willis L. - son of Chas. H. & Rebecca Arno,
  died 20 Mar 1861 at 2 yrs. 6 m.
  Chas. Herbert - son of Chas. H. & Rebecca Arno,
  died 26 Feb 1892 at 24 yrs. 4 m.
  Chas. H. - father, 1834-1914.
  Rebecca - mother, his wife, 1834-1909.
LIBBY, Grace E. - 20 Dec 1876-30 Jul 1895.
  Lavina H. - mother, 4 Mar 1847-1 Jun 1884.
  Freddie - age 9 m.   )Children of L. H. &
  Annie - age 7 d.   )F. Libby.
TIBBETTS, Ephraim T. - died 1 Sep 1919 at 89 yrs.
  Dollie R. - wife of Ephraim T. Tibbetts, died
  6 Feb 1901 at 67 yrs.
CURTIS, Angier H. - 1869-1922.
  Lillian B. Tibbetts - his wife, 1870-1922.
TIBBETTS, Jesse, Dea. - died 21 Jun 1885 at 84
  yrs.
  Wives of Dea. Jesse Tibbetts
  Eliza - died 20 Apr 1829 at 26 yrs.
  Martha - died 13 Apr 1858 at 57 yrs.
BOYNTON, Bessie M. - wife of George F. Boynton,
  1890-1940 (on Tibbetts lot and stone).
WILLIAMS, Emery E. - born 26 Jun 1866, died 21
  Mar 1877.
  John M. - born 21 Jun 1875-
  Melvin H. - 1835-1913.
  Clara H. - wife of M. H. Williams, 1841-1867.
  Fannie Coombs - wife of M. H. Williams, 1845-
  1929.
HIGGINS, Alice R. - wife of William T. Higgins,
  died 7 Aug 1865 at 47 yrs.
THOMPSON, Mary A. - wife of John H. Thompson,
  died 28 Aug 1870 at 26 yrs. 5 m. 9 d.
HIGGINS, Amanda M. - wife of B. Franklin Higgins,
  died 27 Nov 1865 in Lisbon, ME at 32 yrs. 5 m.
  20 d.

Sarah S. - wife of Franklin Higgins, died 27 Dec 1859 at 37 yrs.

SAWYER, Curtis G. - born in Raymond 3 Dec 1827, died in Bowdoinham 8 Oct 1896.

Hannah D. Higgins - wife of Curtis G. Sawyer, born in Webster 19 Nov 1830, died in Lisbon 26 Jan 1868.

Susan O. Higgins - wife of C. G. Sawyer, born 9 Mar 1830, died 17 Dec 1901.

KELLEY, Mary E. Higgins - wife of M. M. Kelley, born in Lisbon 25 May 1847, died in Somerville, Mass. 20 Feb 1835.

SAWYER, Moses H. - born in Lisbon 12 Apr 1789, died in Lisbon 12 Jul 1878.

Elizabeth Tibbetts - his wife, born in Brunswick 15 Jan 1794, died in Lisbon 24 Dec 1875.

James A. - born in Raymond 4 Jan 1823, died in Lisbon 10 Apr 1842.

HATHORN, Wm. H. - born in Boston, MA, 5 Jun 1861, died in Lisbon 29 Mar 1881.

STUART, Ellen - wife of J. O. Stuart & dau of Boynton & Sabra Jones, died 21 Aug 1874 at 27 yrs. 5 m.

JONES, Boyanton - died 7 Jan 1893 at 84 yrs. 11 m.

Sabra - wife of Boyanton, died 13 Jul 1882 at 73 yrs.

PATTERSON, Foster R. - died 23 Feb 1884 at 26 yrs. 3 m.

Thomas R. - died 12 Oct 1906 at 82 yrs.

Martha J. - his wife, died 18 Jan 1909 at 83 yrs.

Margaret ("Margie") A. - dau of Thomas R. & Martha J. Patterson, died 9 Sep 1872 at 16 yrs. 5 m.

GAUVIN, Martha N. Grover - mother, wife of Alfred Gauvin, 1888-1963.

HEALY, Theron A. - 1844-1909.

Frances E. Nason - wife of Theron A. Healy, 1844-1922.
Virgil T. - 1872-1956.
Carrie T. - wife of Virgil T. Healy, 1863-1918.
SYLVESTER, Edith - dau of Virgil T. & Carrie T. Healy, 16 Jan-27 Jun 1907.
CHANDLER, Albianna - wife of Edgar C. Chandler, 1868-1901.
BRANN, Marion - (deceased, but no stone and no dates).
ABELL, Oakman S. - 1816-1903.
Almeda C. - 1828-1901.
Cynthia P. - 1818-1902.
George P. - 1848-1891.
ROBERTS, James F. - father, 11 Dec 1897-23 Oct 1968.
Mary L. - mother, 16 May 1901-
BARRETT, Marion L. - dau, 18 Dec 1924-
Roland P. - husband, 10 Jun 1915-
POTTER, Frank B. - 1849-1912.
Joseph S. - 1848-1912.
Benj. R. - died 15 Feb 1900 at 82 yrs. 3 m.
Susan E. - wife of Benj. R. Potter, died 21 Jun 1904 at 76 yrs. 7 m.
John H., Capt. - died 20 Mar 1928 at 76 yrs. 11 m.
Thomas E. - son of Benj. R. & Susan E. Potter, died 9 Aug 1885 at 25 yrs. 4 m.
Rachel Addie - eldest dau of Benj. R. & Susan E. Potter, died 2 Aug 1890 at 24 yrs. 9 m.
Sara F. - 1870-1956.
FRAZIER, Alvin - 1808-1885.
Elizabeth W. - his wife, 1818-1905.
William O. - Lost at sea, 1846-1872.
Charles S. - 1862-1916.
WHITNEY, Emery Oliver - beloved father & grandfather, 20 Jul 1896-26 May 1984.
Thomas T. - 1843-1918.
Alfretta W. - his wife, 1856-1946.

Ray M. - 1893-1893.
Royed A. - 1899-1901.
Uriah - 1813-1889.
Caroline - his wife, 1808-1884.
ALLEN, Lewis T. - died 5 Dec 1921 at 88 yrs. 4 m.
Bertha - wife Lewis T. Allen, died 19 Dec 1898 at 61 yrs. 8 m.
Lavina A. - dau of Lewis T. & Bertha Allen, died 17 May 1880 at 20 yrs. 4 m.
Maria A. - dau of Lewis T. & Bertha Allen, died 23 Jan 1860 at 2 yrs. 4 m. (stone broken).
Harry Elmer - inf. son of Isaac & Eleona Allen, 17 Jul 1894-19 Jul 1894.
Isaac E. - 8 Feb 1873-2 Nov 1947.
WENTWORTH, Wm. H. - born 20 Jul 1841, died 4 Aug 1891.
Eliza M. - wife of Wm. H. Wentworth, born 8 Jul 1842, died 13 Dec 1891.
S. Louisa (dau of Wm. H. & Eliza M. Wentworth), born 4 Jan 1864, died 18 Aug 1865.
COFFIN, Permelia C. - wife of Jesse Coffin, 1856-1933.
Charles H. - son of Jesse and Julia A. Coffin, 1869-1890.
Dellie -)Children of Jesse & Julia A. Coffin
Willie -)(no dates)
Julia A. - wife of Jesse Coffin, 1841-1883.
Jesse - 1841-1902.
WAKEFIELD, Frank - 1852-1906.
POTTER, Carrie W. - 1858-1939 (stone says sister of Frank Wakefield).
JONES, Addie A. - 1856-1907 (metal marker only).
Anna Reed - 1831-1897 (metal marker only).
Boynton, II - 1819-1899 (metal marker only).
SARGENT, Frank S. - 1861-1943 (metal marker only).
Mary E. - 7 Oct 1834-17 Dec 1922.

HOLBROOK, Charles H. - born 16 Aug 1846, died 15 Aug 1920 (GAR marker).
  Abbie M. - his wife, 1848-1935.
RIDEOUT, James K. - 1849-1930.
  Kate - his wife, 1860-1917.
  Sarah - 1845-1880.
  Jacob - 1798-1882.
  Jane - his wife, 1806-1891.
  Their children
  Fairfield - 1841-1860.
  Mary - 1837-1875.
PHINNEY, Elizabeth E. - 1898-1984.
  Otis M. - 1902-1955.
SAWYER, Oscar Louis - 12 May 1907-17 Jun 1972.
  Ruth Healy - his wife, 29 Sep 1900-21 Aug 1965.
  Duane Healy - 19 May 1938-30 Oct 1990.
WILKINSON, Martina ("Mickey") Lynn - 12 Aug 1949-31 Oct 1972.
HEALY, Harold Eugene - 16 Jan 1899-17 Mar 1974.
  Annette Pelletier - his wife, 20 Jan 1901-11 Apr 1961.
CORNISH
  Infants
  Randall Scott - 1958 (cem records 11 Jun).
  Cynthia Joy - 1960 (cem records 26 Apr).
  Elizabeth E. - 1929-   .
  Herbert W. - 1923-   .
HOLBROOK, John K. - died 19 Mar 1902 at 82 yrs. 2 m.
  Nancy J. - wife of John K. Holbrook, died 9 Nov 1907 at 68 yrs. 5 m.
GOSS, Ethel B. - 23 Jun 1881-6 Jun 1963.
  Willis E. - 7 Nov 1874-18 Nov 1962.
WILLIAMS, Luella Coombs - 20 Jun 1873-17 Sep 1972.
  Clara Horton - 30 Mar 1879-19 Oct 1940.
  Philip E. - 14 Jan 1883-14 Nov 1979.
DYER, Lydia S. - 10 Aug 1812-5 Aug 1892.

FERRIES, Mary - In memory of my mother, died 19
  May 1907 at 67 yrs.
PRINCE, Solomon P. C. - father, died 16 Nov
  1912 at 79 yrs.
  Margaret H. - mother, wife of Solomon P. C.
  Prince, died 8 May 1920 at 88 yrs.
DOUGHTY, Mehitable - his wife, died 28 Feb
  1906 at 77 yrs.
  Isaac L. - died 2 Oct 1871 at 49 yrs.
SMULLEN, Jerrie H. - died at Matanzas 21 Oct
  1870 at 27 yrs.
  Mehitable G. - mother, wife of Samuel Smullen,
  died 13 Dec 1888 at 79 yrs.
  Samuel - father, died 26 Mar 1888 at 84 yrs.
ELLIOTT, Lizzie H. - wife of Charles E. H.
  Elliott, died 10 Nov 1872 at 22 yrs. 6 m. 10 d.
THOMPSON, Mary A. - wife of John H. Thompson,
  died 28 Aug 1870 at 26 yrs. 5 m. 9 d.
STOREY, Daisy M. - 23 Jul 1882-4 Oct 1952.
WALKER, Esther Doherty - wife, 22 May 1877-16
  Jan 1958.
  Harry E. P. - husband, 22 Feb 1872-23 Oct 1953.
STOVER, Eva Mae Reynolds - wife, 30 Apr 1884-
  9 Nov 1963.
  Daniel A. - husband, 12 May 1882-10 Apr 1968.
HALL, Helen P. - 1895-1932.
  Margaret - infant, 1930-1930.
  Alan F. - 1896-1974.
  Ethel L. - 1904-   .
  Francis S. - 1848-1923.
GARLAND, George W. - father, 22 Sep 1899-29 Apr
  1919.
  Sarah Card - mother, 26 Oct 1891-6 Feb 1978.
  Donald W. - son, 28 May 1917-14 Apr 1977.
SKELTON, Leonard B. - 1864-1938.
  Mary J. - his wife, 1870-1941.
  Harold S. - 1897-1939.
  Willis L. - 1893-1958.

Mona J. - his wife, 1899-1975.
CARD, Alonzo H. - husband, 5 Dec 1911-1 Sep 1989.
  Harriet A. - wife, 9 Jul 1913-   .
PARKER, Cathy B. - dau of Mr. & Mrs. B. Parker, 1944-1965.
CARD, Edward S. - 3 Oct 1883-30 Mar 1962.
  Mary E. - his wife, 19 Feb 1906-4 Dec 1967.
CURRIER, Charles M., Jr. - 10 Mar 1913-
  Ruth Card - wife, 16 Apr 1916-   .
  Winston E. - son, 29 Nov 1934-18 Feb 1986,
  A2C, U. S. Air Force Korea.
CARD, Arthur E. - 26 Jun 1894-3 Jan 1960.
  Edna O. Skelton - his wife, 9 May 1900-29 Dec 1980.
STUART, Philip H. - 1892-1959.
  Margaret E. - his wife, 1894-1944.
  Hazel L. - his wife, 1892-1956.
  Clinton Sheridan - son of Margaret & Philip Stuart, PFC, U. S. Army, World War II, 1912-1977.
WHITE, David W. - 1896-   .
  Grace M. - his wife, 1896-1948.
  Evelyn A. - his wife, 1903-1983.
STEVENS, Raymond H. - 1904-1969.
  Eva E. - his wife, 1907-   .
  Raymond L. - their son, 1926-   .
  Lily M. - his wife, 1925-   .
  Linwood B. - their son, 1948-1949.
WOODSUM, Myra - 1904-1989.
ADAMS, Robert E. - husband, 10 Jun 1911-14 Apr 1969.
BARD, Leon E., Sr. - husband, 16 Jun 1903-5 Jan 1989.
  Agnes F. Card - wife, 17 Jul 1913-8 Apr 1992.
KEENE, Ernest A. - 22 Dec 1861-17 Dec 1949.
KATULA, John M. - husband, 12 Nov 1911-1 May 1986.
  Evelyn - wife, 13 Feb 1907-   .
NUTE, Marshall B. - 21 Feb 1883-

Ethel Lowell - his wife, 21 May 1882-29 Jun 1944 (she mother to Robert E. Adams).
BRANN, Mary E. - dau, 1914-1928.
  Alice M. - mother, 1887-1968.
  Walter L. - father, 1883-1971.
  Walter L., Jr. - 24 Mar 1916-21 Apr 1952.
  Jacqueline L. - 16 Sep 1919-22 Mar 1969.
CRAIG, Philip Bruce - 18 Oct 1942-8 Mar 1971, PA AO1, U. S. Navy, Vietnam.
STEWART, Harry C. - 25 Jul 1888-28 Dec 1982.
  Winnifred M. Loft - 14 Oct 1903-   .
  Harry P. - son, 1935-   .
POOLER, Charles J. - 6 Dec 1887-23 Nov 1966.
  Josephine Demchak - wife of C. L. Pooler, 23 Sep 1913-20 Apr 1964.
  Charles L. - 15 Nov 1911-16 Mar 1979.
CURTIS, Frank R. - father, 8 Feb 1886-10 Oct 1953.
  Myrtle E. Arno - mother, 13 Oct 1900-24 Mar 1983.
  Richard M. - "Rickie," loving son of Richard & Joan, 20 Jul 1974-28 Mar 1982.
GARBOTZ, Frances M. - 1914-1974.
  Walter E. - Sgt, U. S. Army, World War II, Korea, 27 Oct 1912-10 Aug 1990.
MERRILL, George C. - 1906-1962.
  Arlene Curtis - his wife, 1918-1977.
McIVER, Edith C. - wife, 22 May 1926-27 Jul 1973.
  Russell E. - husband, 11 Jan 1925-   .
AMES, Chester L. - husband, 1886-1963.
  Marguerite A. - wife, 1900-   .
SKELTON, Ray H. - father, 17 Jul 1902-31 May 1972.
  Myrtle F. Purington - mother, 9 May 1909- 4 Jul 1977.
BONIN, Pauline E. - 20 Feb 1896-9 Mar 1985.
DARLING, June E. - 1 Aug 1926-15 Oct 1977 (on

Huston lot and "Nellie's sister" on stone).
HUSTON, Nellie M. - mother, 28 Mar 1924-10 Sep 1973.
  Carroll B. - father, 18 Oct 1902-23 Jun 1976.
LAMOREAU, Beverly G. - dau, 21 Oct 1950-25 Mar 1970 (on Huston lot).
INGERSON, Dewey - husband, 5 Apr 1918-
  Phyllis Downes - wife, 3 Sep 1922-4 Aug 1970.
PARKER, Ainsley E., Sr. - father, 11 Jul 1908-25 Nov 1972.
ARNDT, Jack W. - 8 Aug 1922-
  Cynthia Spear - his wife, 21 Jul 1921-
RINES, Jobeth - inf dau of Richard & Karen Rines, 29 Mar 1974.
  Richard L., Sr. - 11 Dec 1928-
  Elizabeth J. - 1 Jan 1930-9 Nov 1989.
MORGAN, Wilfred A. - father, 4 Oct 1913-
  Lydia Mae Woods - mother, 15 Sep 1922-
  Carlene F. Card - wife, 21 Apr 1944-
  Granville H. - husband, 26 Jan 1943-
BICKFORD, Carl A. - born at Lisbon Falls, ME, 28 Jul 1907, son of Horace F. and Allegra (Blaisdell) Bickford, died at Lewiston, ME, 7 Oct 1990.
  Jayne E. Harrington - his wife, born at Burlington, VT, 29 Feb 1924, dau of Edgar Clayton and Vina L. (Farr) Harrington, died at
LITTLEFIELD, George A. - 1895-1978.
  Irma E. Davis - his wife, 1903-1990.
WARD, Louise G. - 1904-1980.
GAUTHIER, Carlene B. Ward - 1926-
  Alcide Cyril - Cpl U. S. Army, World War II, 1919-1976.
  William A. - baby, 12 Oct 1968-13 Dec 1968.
SPEAR, Marion Welsch - wife, 9 May 1917-
  William - husband, 9 Oct 1909-25 Sep 1979.
SMALL, Leslie - husband, 24 Nov 1915-23 Jun 1988.
  Helen Dalrymple - wife, 14 Dec 1914-

CONLEY, Mildred E. - 1905-1960.
  Albert F. - 1903-1989.
RICHARDSON, Bernard O. - 1911-1961.
  Florence M. - 1905-1979.
JOHNSTON, Teresa Lee - beloved dau of Jackie &
  May Johnston, 2 Mar 1959-3 Mar 1959.
HINCKLEY, Gordon Winter, PFC U. S. Army, World
  War 2, 24 Mar 1927-11 May 1978.
  Leon A. - 1905-1958.
  Myra B. - his wife, 1905- .
WAGG, William - Pvt U. S. Army, Co. L, 363 Inf.,
  W. W. I, 2 May 1896-2 Aug 1974.
  Joshua James - 3-17-78 - 3-20-78.
  William H. - son, 28 Jul 1923- .
  Evelyn Bubier - his wife, 30 Dec 1928- .
  Howard J. - son, ME 2, U. S. Navy, 24 Feb
  1930-11 Nov 1952.
  Lola Curtis - his wife, Beloved Momma, 12 Nov
  1930-25 Dec 1985.
LUNT, Howard L.- 1892-1968.
  Ina Jones - his wife, 1894-1987.
PETTIPAS, Marion Lunt - their dau, 1923-1954
  (on Lunt lot).
ROBERTS, Herbert L. - 17 Dec 1905- .
  Frances T. Webber - his wife, 20 Jul 1905-30
  Jan 1950.
CARD, Margaret M. - "Joe," 1923- .
  Frank L. - "Roy," 1913-1987.
  Martha L. - wife, 1883-1973.
  Frank B. - husband, 1877-1966.
SKELTON, Thurman L. - 1918- .
  Marion E. - 1924- .
  Ernest R. - 1949-1950.
ELLINGWOOD, I. Walter (Isaac Walter, but always
  known as "Walter I."), 1 Sep 1873-8 Jul 1954.
  Carrie Greene - his wife, 19 May 1883-7 Sep
  1950.

MICHAUD, Ronald L. - Cpl. U. S. Army Korea, 26 May 1926-23 Apr 1983.
  Estelle - wife, 18 Oct 1896-21 Sep 1971.
  Onesime - father, 17 Apr 1894-25 Jan 1954.
MORNEAU, Marie A. - mother, 4 Mar 1887-22 Dec 1949.
  Amedee - father, 25 Feb 1870-6 Mar 1951.
COSKERY, Charles F. - 1920-1977.
  Baby - 2 Feb 1946.
PROUT, Harry E. - 22 Apr 1879-28 Aug 1943.
  Bessie M. - 27 Jan 1880-4 Sep 1946.
GREENE, Charles S. - 1856-1936 (monument), 4 Feb 1856-26 Sep 1935 (other stone).
  Lillian Rose Nay - his wife, 7 Sep 1864-16 Apr 1947.
  Percy C. - 1 Oct 1885-2 May 1971.
GILBERT, Olive - mother, 1874-1944.
WAGG, Geraldine Theresa - 4-19-25-4-5-88 (dau of Emery Oliver Whitney).
STEWART, Calvin B. - husband, 1915-
  Dorothy C. - wife, 1921-1989.
  Carole Ann - dau, 1939-1940.
ARNO, John W. - 20 Apr 1860-3 Jan 1938.
  Effie D. - 8 Jan 1870-20 Jan 1945.
LAMB, Leola B. - 26 Jun 1895-27 Jun 1957.
MacKENZIE, Elsie M. - 16 Sep 1892-12 Apr 1988.
KEITH, Royce E. - son, 1939-1990.
  Elmer L. - husband, 1912-1989.
  Dorothy E. - wife, 1907-1982.
  Kenneth Elmer - baby, 1938-1938.
LIBBY, Rena L. Arno - 1897-1976.
NASON, Susie R. Arno - 24 Dec 1898-4 Dec 1984.
ARNO, Sarah E. Clark - wife of Berley M. Arno, 16 Aug 1877-14 Nov 1952.
  Berley M. - 17 Jul 1870-7 Oct 1935.
WEBBER, Henry M. - 2 Mar 1871-10 May 1965.
  Fannie Alice Townsend - wife of Henry M. Webber, 24 Aug 1874-20 Sep 1968.

Dwight F. - their son, 4 Jun 1899-8 Mar 1964.
  Hulda Jones - his wife, 18 Apr 1896-22 Nov 1940 (another stone, 1895).
  Carrie E. - 11 Jan 1863-21 May 1933.
  Lawrence E. - husband, 1903-   .
  Helen F. Gustin - wife, 1901-1990.
COOMBS, Bernard H. - born 1 Apr 1906, died 16 Aug 1937.
  Daniel A. - 1850-1938.
  Matilda - 1881-1970.
COSKERY, Helen M. - 27 Aug 1922-25 May 1943.
  Lenora - 1889-1961.
  Frank - 1891-1980 (World War I marker).
GILLESPIE, George L.-2 Dec 1875-4 Jan 1961.
  Nettie M. (per cemetery records, May) - his wife, 15 Dec 1884-31 Dec 1968.
BAILEY, Carleton E. - 1920-1984.
  Jesse P. - 1868-1938.
  Anna E. MacLean - his wife, 1873-1929.
  William M. - 1898-1974.
  Bessie M. - his wife, 1903-1946.
WILLIAMS, John L. - 1840-1924.
  Martha W. - his wife, 1842-1917.
  Henry B. - 1875-1916.
  Mary E. - 1879-1969.
SPEAR, Fannie C. - mother, 1856-1935.
PARRIS, Pearl Vernon - 1904-1908.
WALKER, Lola A. - dau, 18 Mar 1906-5 Apr 1992 (on Polley lot).
POLLEY, Charles P. - son, 10 Nov 1903-14 Aug 1972.
  William L. - father, 24 Dec 1866-8 May 1948.
  Eva A. - mother, 11 Mar 1882-24 Jan 1970.
  Hazel E. - dau, 23 Dec 1900-3 Jun 1902.
GOSS, Philip W. - 1908-1911 (funeral home marker).
  Irvin W. - 1869-1930.
  Leora E. - 1881-1919.

AMES, J. A. - 1849-1928.
  Narcissa M. - his wife, died 15 Aug 1911 at 61 yrs. 21 d.
  Carrie M. Wentworth - mother, 1875-1921.
  Enola - died 11 Apr 1909 at 32 yrs. 8 m. 18 d.
WHEELER, Lincoln C. - 1868-1945.
  Della Arno - his wife, 1873-1936.
MARR, Augustine - 1854-1918.
  Eva M. Arno - his wife, 1862-1921.
BICKFORD, Horace F. - 1882-1947.
  Allegra Blaisdell - wife of Horace Bickford, 1882-1979.
  H. Lloyd - 1911-1922 (son of Horace and Allegra).
  Frank P. - 1855-1941.
  Emily A. - his wife, 1861-1935.
  Leslie G. - 1 Nov 1891-17 Apr 1988.
  Daisy Greene - 13 Jun 1888-7 Aug 1963 (wife of Leslie)
  Kenneth R. - 2 Jul 1917-27 Jan 1983.
  Janice Carolyn - dau, 12 Sep 1923-13 Jan 1924.
  Infant Son - died 13 Apr 1925 (Norman).
  (Kenneth through Infant, children of Leslie and Daisy.)
WILLIAMS, Charles - 1 Aug 1856-6 Nov 1935.
  Addie - his wife, 29 Sep 1859-22 Feb 1927.
TARR, Melvin - 1866-1933.
HAIGH, Harry - 27 Nov 1885-16 Sep 1959.
  Jennie M. Curtis - his wife, 16 Sep 1882-24 Nov 1928.
  Their grandson
TOWLE, Baby Russell Dale - born and died 6 Nov 1939.
JONES, Bert L. - 1864-1933.
  Gertrude Arno - his wife, 1865-1942.
  Ira V. - 1886-1955.
ROBERTS, Cora E. - 1901-1979.
BURTON, Clifford E. - 1904-1935.

WALKER, Jay A. - husband, 1897-1954 (W. W. I).
  Marion - wife, 1901-1975.
FOWLER, Carrie O. Brocklebank - 1904-   .
  James E. - 1901-   .
EMOND, Ronald B. - 27 Jun 1951-1 Aug 1968.
BLICK, Ernest E. - husband, 14 Jun 1908-27 Oct
  1969.
  Alice M. - died 2 Aug 1979 at 67 yrs. (no
  stone but in cemetery records).
PELKEY, Leslie J. - 1896-1969.
  Nina E. Shorette - 1906-   , his wife.
McINTIRE, Alma M. - 7 Jan 1896-19 Apr 1971.
  James R. - 25 Feb 1896-23 May 1974.
ROBERTS, Theodore A. - husband, Maine PFC BTRY B
  158 FA BN World War II, 16 Nov 1921-18 Feb
  1973.
  Elizabeth M. - wife, 1928-   .
NELSON, Gladys M. - 1894-1979, wife of Arthur
  F. Nelson.
  Arthur F. - husband of Gladys M. Nelson, 1889-
  1980.
ADAMS, Clyde T. - husband of Blanche E. Adams,
  28 Mar 1902-12 Jul 1982.
  Blanche E. - wife of Clyde T. Adams, 30 Jan
  1898-16 Jan 1988.
COOMBS, Albert M. - 1834-1907.
  Sarah E. - wife of A. M. Coombs, 1836-1901.
  Ernest M. - inf son, 1870-1870.
HIGGINS, Daniel H. - father, died 21 Feb 1899
  at 74 yrs. 10 m.
  Mahala A. - his wife, died 15 Jan 1905 at 78
  yrs. 3 m.
SALLEY, George H., Rev. - 12 May 1869-13 Feb
  1911.
  Ida A. M. - wife of George H. Salley, died 9
  Jul 1907 at 36 yrs. 8 m. 26 d.
WILLIAMS, Ralph - 1884-1911.
  Arthur G. - 1877-1943.

   Margaret Simmons - his wife, 1864-1953.
   Bessie - wife of A. G. Williams, 1875-1904.
CURTIS, Nehemiah - GAR 1861-1865, Co. F, 24th ME Vol., 1838-1925.
   Rachel - his wife, 1850-1919.
   Fred E. - 1876-1911.   ) Their
OLDHAM, Annie - 1872-1918.) children
WALES, William G. - 1879-1959.
   Lyda B. Clark - his wife, 1879-1971.
CLARK, Anson M. - 1853-1922.
   Mary E. - 1850-1881.) His
   Lizzie C. - 1859-1920.) wives
   Louis N. - 1855-1884.
RAND, Thomas R. - died 13 Dec 1909 at 82 yrs. 3 m.
   Climena W. - wife of Thomas R. Rand, died 11 Dec 1911 at 81 yrs. 8 m. 28 d.
GRAY, Nathaniel C. - 1852-1925.
   Lilla Fry - his wife, 1857-1937.
   George W. - 1865-1904.
   Anne P. Clark - his wife, 1867-1896.
   Marshall A. - their son, 1894-1982 (3 May 1982 per cemetery records).
CARD, James G. - 1888-1961 (there is a funeral home marker for S. G. Card and the same dates and no S. G. Card in the cemetery records).
   Grace Coskery - his wife, 1902-
   Bertha E. - 1932-1932.
   Forest W. - 1934-1934. Children
DECOVIN, Elenora Allen - 1879-1948.
   John H. - 1839-1913.
ALLEN, Edward -) No stones but in
MUMFORD, James -) cemetery records.
HIGGINS, Herbert D. - 1879-1956 (cemetery records show 7 Jun 1956).
   Lizzie D. - 1896-   (cemetery records show date of death as 10 May 1986).

Andrew D. - 1913-1914.
O'GRADY, James - Co. I, 7th U. S. Inf., born at Rouses Point, Lake Champlain, N. Y., 2 Aug 1850 (no date of death).
 Amy Maria - his wife, born at Chazy, N. Y., 29 Sep 1851, died 4 Nov 1937.
PRINCE, Arlon P. - father, 1869-1944.
 Amanda Jordan - mother, his wife, 1897-1979 (cemetery records 21 Aug 1979).
 Albert S. - 1921-1921.
 Linwood K. - 1920-1971 (cemetery records 8 Jun 1971 at 51 yrs.).
 Margaret P. - 1916- .
GROSS, Frank O. - 18 Jul 1906- .
 Madeline L. Pooler - his wife, 31 Jan 1905- .
POOLER, John A. - 25 Aug 1869-16 Mar 1934.
 Millie A. Chandler - his wife, 23 Jun 1874-1 Apr 1917.
 Earl C. - their son, 16 Sep 1907-21 Nov 1932.
SMITH, Samuel L. - 3 Dec 1858-9 Jun 1933.
 Annette L. Jones - his wife, 16 Nov 1858-4 Jan 1934.
SMALL, Albert P. - 1854-1938.
 Mary E. Snell - his wife, 1860-1917.
JORDAN, Bertius L. - 1869-1926.
 Mary E. - his wife, 1865-1932.
 Emma A. - 1901-1926.
 Bertius L., Jr. -CWT U. S. Navy World Wars I and II, 2 Dec 1898-24 Sep 1990.
 Elsie J. - wife, 17 May 1905-25 May 1987.
 Fred E. - MM1 U. S. Navy Korea, 2 Oct 1933-28 Sep 1976.
 Mary M. - wife, 1941- .
 Ellery B. - PFC U. S. Marine Corps, 18 Oct 1937-31 Jul 1983.
 Carol A. - wife, 1933- .
SMITH, Frank H. - 1864-1926.
 Nellie A. - his wife, 1862-1926.

Harry G. - their grandson, 1923-1926.
WILLIAMS, George E. - 1869-1954.
  Elizabeth Potter - his wife, 1867-1949.
  Grace Small - 1890-1944.
UPHAM, J. Randall - 1906-1991.
  Frances Williams - his wife, 1898-
KEAY, Merrill G. - 1857-1928.
  Benja E. - his wife, 1861-1943.
  Norman L. - son, 1885-1885.
  Mabel O. - dau, 1889-1933.
ANDERSON, Alexander G. - 1885-1976 (cemetery record 11 Sep 1976 at 90 yrs.).
  Helen K. - his wife, 1897-1968 (cemetery record 3 Jan 1968 at 70 yrs.).
  Newman G. - 1925-
  Barbara H. - his wife, 1944-
ROLLISON, Lois Jean A. - born 9 Mar 1944, died 17 Oct 1977 (grandchild of Alexander and Helen Anderson).
TARR, Richard W. - 1899-1964.
  Florence E. Cornish - his wife, 1902-1929.
  Their infant son - 1929-1929.
  Ruth - his wife, 1905-1983.
COX, Eva - 1895-1951.
CORNISH, Joseph W. - 1862-1932.
  Angeline Delaney - his wife, 1867-1942.
  Harry J. - 1895-1958.
  Gladys C. - his wife, 1896-1989.
HARMON, Vernon F. - father, 21 Jun 1908-
  Hazel B. - mother, 18 Nov 1909-31 Jan 1988.
  Larry A. - son, 20 Jul 1949-21 Jun 1962.
  Purlie E. - father, 28 Jan 1881-5 Dec 1970.
FOWLER, Harriet M. Tarr - wife of Willis A. Fowler, 2 Sep 1922-
  Willis A. - TEC5, U. S. Army, World War II, 15 Jan 1918-29 Jun 1979.
JONES, Ruth A. - 29 Mar 1895-11 Jan 1992.
CORNISH, James T. - 8 Feb 1885-12 Nov 1956.

Hannah Hill - his wife, 30 Jan 1888-7 Dec 1971.
TARR, Josephine M. - wife, 1926-1966 (cemetery records 16 Jun 1966).
Kenneth J. - husband, 1923-1983 (cemetery records 18 Nov 1983 - World War II marker).
Kristina Rae - 22 Nov 1979-31 May 1980.
FOWLER, Alton O. - father, 1930- .
Raylene M. - mother, 1934-1974.
ST. AMANT, Richard N. - SP 4 U. S. Army, 6 Dec 1937-4 Feb 1984.
BEAL, Annie E. Reynolds - mother, 1910-1979.
Clarence O. - father, 1909-1980.
REYNOLDS, Ralph R. - father, 1908-1982.
Lillian F. - mother, 1914-1978.
REED, David A. - 1911-1989.
Viola M. - wife, 1923-1992.
Mary J. - dau, 1949- .
KIMBLER, Blanche J. - 12 Apr 1926-9 Jun 1976.
CARD, Harry M. - 1921- .
Abby E. B. Stover - his wife, 1931- .
Harry M., Jr. - 1953- , son.
PULK, Arthur J. - 1905-1982.
Josephine N. - 1911- .
MAXWELL, Charles P. - 30 Jul 1848-27 Aug 1914.
Annie S. - his wife, 4 Oct 1848-10 Oct 1907.
WILSON, James T. - 29 Nov 1859-23 Apr 1908.
Hattie H. - his wife, 11 May 1847-27 Nov 1918.
MAXWELL, Charles H. - 18 Jan 1877-20 Mar 1911.
Ursula M. - his wife, 2 Apr 1879-26 Jul 1968.
HEALY, Abraham H. - born in Fall River, Mass., 29 Apr 1810, died in Lisbon, ME, 1 Mar 1867.
Nancy Coombs - his wife, born in Bowdoin, ME, 21 May 1812, died in Bowdoin, ME, 2 Jun 1876.
Wm. Ferdinand - their son, born 14 Feb 1848, died 18 Sep 1852.
PURINTON, Alonzo - born in Bowdoin, ME, 20 Sep 1847, died in Bowdoin, ME, 24 Aug 1916.

Emma A. Healy - his wife, born in Lisbon, ME, 16 Mar 1852, died in Bowdoin, ME, 2 Dec 1920.
Frank - 1857-1909.
Abbie M. - 1860-1941.
Nathaniel S. - 24 Feb 1844-1 Jun 1908.
Jennie E. Williams - his wife, 12 May 1843-7 Apr 1916.
Lester Given, M. D. - 28 Mar 1873-13 Nov 1903.
Newman Albert - 2 Nov 1882-10 Apr 1901.
Henry - 1869-1936.
Ellen - his wife, 1855-1925.
SPRINGER, Frances P. - 1875-1907 (on Purinton lot).
NOWELL, William H. - died 27 May 1901 at 47 yrs. 2 m.
Harriet E. - his wife, died 1 Nov 1937 at 85 yrs. 11 m.
Jeremiah - 1811-1879.
Anstrice M. - his wife, 1820-1892.
Cora E. - their dau, 1861-1863.
CARD, James W. - father, 19 Oct 1847-1 Jun 1914.
Minerva Benson - mother, 30 Sep 1860-19 Nov 1949.
Hattie C. - dau, 17 Dec 1896-16 Dec 1909.
Harry M. - son, 9 Sep 1885-24 Jan 1913.
Clifford L. - son, 4 May 1902-10 Jan 1914.
Alonzo P. - husband of Edna M. Starbird, 4 Jul 1880-3 Jan 1909.
Leighton A. - son, 24 Nov 1906-24 Nov 1906.
Clyde J. - son, 11 Dec 1907-1 Mar 1909.
JONES, Edna M. Starbird - wife of J. Everett Jones, 19 Dec 1886-24 Mar 1961.
J. Everett - husband of Edna M. Starbird, 3 Sep 1889-28 Nov 1971.
LOWELL, Uriah - 1832-1904.
Mahala D. - his wife, 1856-1940.
Dorothy E. - 1904-
Laurence U. - 1898-1960.

POOLER, Mabel L. - 1880-1973.
GAGNON, Joseph A., Jr. - 1902-1947.
COTTON, William S. - 1851-1909.
  Hattie M. - his wife, 1853-1916.
STONE, Adna N. - 1839-1917.
  Sarah E. - his wife, 1846-1938.
  Ruth E. - 1890-1913.
  Stephen P. - 1872-1955.
  Isaac M. - 1875-   (cemetery records died 5 May 1964).
PROUT, Lendall A. - 1848-1924.
  Ida May Stinchfield - his wife, 1857-1939.
GROVER, James L. - 1906-1913 (on Prout lot).
PROUT, Herbert L. - 1862-1945.
PARKER, Lena Prout - 1885-1927.
PROUT, John - (no stone but in cemetery records).
PURINGTON, Claramae - 1890-1965.
PURINTON, Chas. W., Rev. - 1849-1910.
  Hattie N. - 1860-1942.
  Preston, Sr. - U. S. Army, World War II, 15 Aug 1916-18 Mar 1988.
  Marion - (wife of Preston Purinton), 1918-1972.
  Ray - 1883-1954.
  Richard - 18 Oct 1917-   .
  Audrey R. Mitchell - his wife, 10 Jun 1926-3 Mar 1990.
DOUGHTY, John H. - 8 Aug 1862-11 Aug 1952.
  Etta M. - 7 Jul 1867-19 Jul 1952.
  John H., Jr. - 19 Aug 1899-   .
  Ina Hicks - 18 Jul 1900-3 Mar 1987.
NOWELL, Walter L. - 1882-1964.
  Mary B. Pick - his wife, 1876-1962.
MANTER, Wayne - father, 9 Oct 1914-7 Jul 1957.
  Greta E. - mother, 5 Feb 1906-
  Patricia M. - inf. dau, died 14 May 1942.
BARNES, Laurence J. - son, 6 Apr 1904-2 Sep 1904.
  Grace M. - mother, 18 Oct 1883-26 May 1977.
  John B. - father, 25 Jul 1851-6 Jul 1935.

LIDBACK, Edward B. - 1879-1958.
  Lila D. - 1892-1986.
DOUGHTY, Dorothy J. - 6 Dec 1927-12 Aug 1980.
  John H., III - 21 Feb 1923-
           (Married) 24 Aug 1946
  Jamie - inf., 7-25-73 9-6-73.
WILLIAMS, Guy M. - 16 Dec 1881-18 Apr 1958.
  Nellie M. Bickford - his wife, 13 May 1904-
  Lewis E. - bro of Guy M. & Gracie E., 31 May
  1884-3 Jul 1946.
TAYLOR, Wilbur B. - 4 May 1905-
  Gracie E. Williams - his wife, 11 Sep 1895-
  27 Oct 1950.
YOUNG, Larry Wayne - beloved son of Mary L.
  Small and Lewis S. Young, 6 Apr 1944-15 Apr
  1956.
  Shirley Lewis - PFC U. S. Army, WW II, 17 May
  1920-24 May 1989.
  Mary L. Small - wife of S. Lewis Young, 20
  Jan 1920-   , married 5 Nov 1938.
  Victoria Beote - his wife, 8 Apr 1883-28 Nov
  1963. (Per family member, "Victorine" is
  name on birth record.)
  Lucius A. - 30 Aug 1887-23 Apr 1968, married
  1 Sep 1906.
SMALL, Joel U. - 1940-1964.
  Harold James - ME Pvt. 1 Co. 151 Depot Brig.
  WW 1, 14 Sep 1889-2 Aug 1971.
BUTTERICK, Harry "Bruce" - S1 U. S. Navy, WW II,
  1 Jan 1927-5 Nov 1989.
  Helen Frances Small - 1923-
HARMON, Mark J. - Our Beloved Son, 1961-1969.
OWEN, Maurice E. - husband, father, 3 Mar 1910-
  3 Dec 1987.
  Laura E. - wife, mother, 8 Mar 1921-
  Richard W. - son, 13 Dec 1948-22 Feb 1966.
BYRAS, Evelyn L. McKinney - mother, wife of
  George D. Byras, 7 Mar 1935-6 Nov 1967.

George D. - father, 22 Dec 1931- .
Arlene Gail - 1953-1971 (there is apparently an unmarked grave on this lot).
McKINNEY, James L. - 1910- .
Frances O. Collins - his wife, 1914-1970.
SAVAGE, N. Ricky - 1961-1977.
RANCOURT, George R. - 1916- .
Lois E. Prince - his wife, 1918- .
MILLIKEN, Dorothy L. R. - their (Geo. & Lois Rancourt) dau, AMN U. S. Air Force Viet Nam, 5 Jul 1949-6 Jul 1976.
McINTIRE, Ralph G. - m. 27 Aug 1948, 22 Apr 1929- .
Anne C. Pelkey - his wife, 22 Aug 1931-9 Aug 1988.
KING, Harold J. - PFC U. S. Army WW II, 7 Apr 1910-11 May 1977.
Marie J. - his wife, 1914- .
MERRILL, Dwight E. - 1903-1978.
Anna H. - 1903-1986.
TARR, O. Clyde, Jr. - 3-13-59 - 6-17-78.
WOODS, William A. - husband, 1912- .
Eva N. - wife, 1913- .
BARTLETT, Claire L. Ward - 1942-1981.
RUSSELL, Herbert W. - Cpl. U. S. Army WW II, 11 Jun 1912-20 Apr 1982.
Emma C. - his wife, 15 Apr 1924- .
CORNISH, Lilyette Bernier - mother, 11 Mar 1934-.
Mark Stanley - son, 12 Aug 1966-2 Sep 1988.
BERNIER, Arlene F. - 4 Mar 1951-12 Feb 1984.
Paul P., Sr. - 16 Jan 1947- .
REED, Shane A. - 1985-1985.
SMALL, Carroll Charles, Jr. - S1 U. S. Navy, World War II, 30 Sep 1925-5 May 1983.
Katherine Elizabeth Byras - his wife, 29 Aug 1928- , married 30 Oct 1948.
CALLEN, Rodney J. - 30 Nov 1953- .

Sarah "Sam" - 8 Jul 1988-18 May 1990.
   Mary A. - 11 Aug 1951-
FELDMAN, Rachel Elizabeth - dau, 1979-1990.
BERNIER - married 18 Sep 1933.
   George E. - 27 Feb 1911-17 Dec 1989.
   Jeanette - 19 Apr 1912-
   Jeanette L. - 7 Sep 1940-8 Oct 1947.
SAWYER, William E. - 30 Oct 1949-
   Beverly R. Skelton - his wife, 23 May 1952-
GOWELL, Paul E. - EMC U. S. Navy, 14 Jul 1942-
   8 Feb 1991.
   Elaine E. Skelton - his wife, 27 Aug 1947-
RINGROSE, Walter R. - GM2 U. S. Navy World War
   II-Korea-Viet Nam, 16 Jan 1926-22 Apr 1988.
   Joan Roberts - his wife, 1952-
LAMBERT, Tiffany Jo - 1991-1991.
PATRICK, Kenneth L. - 30 Aug 1917-
SKELTON, Dorothy - 29 Jan 1943-21 Feb 1987.
BLICK, Warren J. - A1C U. S. Air Force Korea,
   29 Nov 1935-20 Apr 1985.
MAHER, Donald F. - PFC U. S. Army WW II, 22
   Dec 1917-27 Dec 1983.
   Katherine - 1916-
DURICKO, Michael J., Sr. - S1 U. S. Navy WW II,
   25 Mar 1924-3 Jun 1979.
   Alice M. - 1930-
DANA, Irma P. Welsch - 10 May 1908-
   David Winterburn - 14 Jan 1906-
   (Dana stones are on Wm. Spear lot.)

Woodlawn Cemetery - to go to this cemetery, follow directions for West Bowdoin Cemetery on page 27 and continue 1 mile further. Woodlawn is on the same side of the road as West Bowdoin Cemetery. These inscriptions were copied in the late 1970's with some additions as late as 1992.

GALUSHA, Melville Butler - son of Ebenezer & Lucy Galusha, died 28 Jul 1847 at 12 yrs. 5 m.
  Esther Ann - dau of Eben & Lucy Galusha died (dates buried but 21 in 1850 Census).
BOOBIER, Artemus W. - Co. A 12th ME Vols War of 1861, died 10 Sep 1880 at 38 yrs. 2 m. 19 d.
GALLUSHA, Lucy - wife of Eben.^{r}, died 31 Oct 1856 at 49 yrs. 10 m. Her price is above rubies.
  Joseph - died 15 Feb 1849 at 76 yrs. 3 m.
BUBIER, John - died 14 Jun 1859 at 36 yrs. 6 m. 23 d.

  A Husband kind - a Father dear,
  Serenely sleeps in silence here,
  He lived in peace--in peace he died,
  For Christ his Saviour was his guide.

BUBERE, Hannah, Mrs. - wife of Andrew Bubere, died 30 Mar 1841 at 50 yrs.
  Andrew - died 24 Feb 1852 at 51 yrs. 10 m.
GALUSHA, Lydia Bubier - wife of Elijah Galusha, died 1 Feb 1884 at 79 yrs. 5 m.
RING, Nancy C. - dau of Thomas & Dorcas Ring, died 6 Mar 1850 at 22 yrs.
GOOLD, Maria A. - wife of Harvy M. Goold, died 10 Jan 1850 at 24 yrs.
  William H. - their son, died 1 Aug 1848 at 4 wks.

RING, Isaac B. - Co F 24th ME Vols, 6 Aug 1834-
20 Feb 1914 (GAR marker).
  Dorcas - wife of Thomas Ring, died 14 Nov 1865
  at 86 yrs.
  Thomas - died 5 Dec 1855 at 74 yrs.
JENKINS, Mary - dau of Isaac & Martha Jenkins,
  died 10 Jun 1854 (stone broken and balance
  of inscription not readable; however, <u>Bowdoin
  Vital Records</u>, Vol. II, edited by Rachel
  Townsend Cox, says at 15 y. 5 m. 10 d.).
  Martha A. - dau of Isaac & Martha Jenkins,
  died 25 Sep 1851 at 14 yrs. 9 d.
  Martha - wife of Isaac Jenkins, Esq, died 8
  Nov 1855 at 46 yrs. 6 m. 6 d.
  Isaac - (according to <u>Bowdoin Vital Records</u>,
  Isaac, husband of Martha, died Bowdoin 1834;
  no burial place given. However, due to age
  of daus at death, it appears 1834 is an in-
  correct date of death).
COOMBS, Lavina Carr - Missionary To India For
  Forty Years 1882-1922, 1849-1927.
  David E. - son of David & Sarah Coombs, Lost
  at Sea 29 Oct 1867 at 37 yrs. 3 m.
  George A. - son of David & Sarah Coombs,
  Lost at Sea 29 Oct 1867 at 21 yrs. 2 m.
  James M. - son of David & Sarah Coombs was
  lost at sea 28 Sep 1852 at 25 yrs. 6 m.

  On Arklow bank, near Ireland's coast,
  The ship Mobile and crew were lost;
  And one of them was James our son,
  Lord, help us say thy will be done.

  Lincoln Patten - son of David & Sarah Coombs,
  died 13 Aug 1847 at 6 yrs.
  Sarah - wife of Capt David Coombs, died 9 Feb
  1879 at 74 yrs.
  David, Capt. - died 24 Apr 1856 at 53 yrs.

Brown - died 1 May 1879 at 76 yrs.
Harriet S. - his wife, died 28 Dec 1893 at 83 yrs.
David M. - died at Bath 1870 at 42 yrs.
Dennis B. - died 3 Mar 1850 at 11 d.
Frances M. - died 14 Feb 1885 at 53 yrs.
Harriet J. - 1839-1897.
Zebulon - 1834-1907.
Nancy H. - 1838-1913.

STUART, Melisia A. - dau of Andrew & Rachel Stuart, died 10 Apr 1872 at 13 yrs. 6 m.
Rachel - mother, wife of Andrew J. Stewart died 1 Nov 1885 at 67 yrs.
Joseph - died 28 Jun 1852 at 61 yrs. 9 m.
_appy - died 13 May 1866 at 88 yrs. 11 m. (Bowdoin Vital Records Happy w. of Joseph).

STEWART, Andrew J. - died 26 Aug 1887 at 63 yrs. 3 m.

TEMPLE, Margaret E. - dau of Ivory & Rebecca Temple, died 25 Aug 1852 at 2 yrs. 1 m.
Children of Ivory and Rebecca Temple
Joseph - died 1 Sep 1852 at 8 yrs. 9 m.
Ivory - died 2 Sep 1852 at 5 yrs. 10 m.
Mary E. - died 29 Sep 1842 at 2 yrs.
Rebecca J. - died 27 Sep 1842 at 6 m.
Rachel M. - died 21 Sep 1842 at 4 yrs.
Margaret - died 16 Sep 1842 at 7 yrs.
Ivory - died 9 Sep 1852 at 45 yrs. 4 m.

STEWART, Lovina R. - dau of Samuel & Esther A. Stewart, died 28 Sep 1858 at 1 yr. 1 m.

TEMPLE, Miranda A. - dau of Joseph & Betsey Temple, born 16 Jun 1835 (no date of death).

NILES, Fannie T. - sister, wife of Frederick Niles, born 25 Apr 1810, died 27 Jun 1891 (on Temple lot).

TEMPLE, Joseph - father, died 9 Jun 1882 at 95 yrs. 7 m. 27 d.
Betsey R. - mother, beloved wife of Joseph Temple, died 15 Oct 1885 at 97 yrs. 2 m. 1 d.

PURVES, Thomas L. - 5 May 1832-16 Nov 1915.
  Eleanor M. - 21 Feb 1831-14 Mar 1924.
COOMBS, Gertrude Purves - 23 Jul 1868-9 Oct 1964.
  Charles W. - 19 Sep 1866-24 Jul 1924.
  Emily J. - 29 Nov 1832-24 Feb 1906.
  John D. - 5 Aug 1837-22 May 1888.
TARR, Joseph - died 14 Apr 1906 at 76 yrs. 11 m. 6 d.
  Hannah E. - wife of Joseph Tarr, died 20 Aug 1886 at 44 yrs. 9 m. 9 d.
HOLBROOK, Mary E. - dau of Arthur and Margery Holbrook, died 20 Jul 1870 at 21 yrs.
BOOKER, Hannah - died 21 Apr 1871 at 79 yrs. 6 m.
  Mary - wife of Daniel Booker, died 30 Jan 1844 at 80 yrs. 9 m.
  Daniel - died 8 Nov 1856 at 97 yrs (Revolutionary marker).
RIDEOUT, Elijah - died 16 May 1893 at 77 yrs. 8 m.
  Amanda M. - wife of Elijah Rideout, died 2 Nov 1863 at 35 yrs. 15 d.
ALLEN, Sarah F. - dau of Joel and Louisa, died 7 Sep 1863 at 20 yrs. 8 m.

We laid her in the lonely grave,
When life had just begun
We yield her up to God who gave,
And say, thy will be done.

  Joel - died 4 May 1887 at 79 yrs. 6 m. 24 d.
  Louisa A. - wife of Joel Allen, died 5 Feb 1884 at 76 yrs. 5 m. 23 d.
JONES, Anna - the faithful mother of ten children, departed this life 12 Mar 1861 at 58 yrs.
OLIVER, Julia A. - wife of William S. Oliver, 25 Jul 1834-23 May 1913.
GETCHELL, Olive S. - wife of James L. Getchell, died 30 Dec 1842 at 32 yrs. 8 m.

GATCHELL, James L. - died 12 Aug 1898 at 90 yrs.
  Elizabeth - wife of James L. Gatchell, died
  24 Sep 1904 at 77 yrs. 8 m.
  Charles - son of James L. & Olive S. Getchell,
  died 1 Jan 1854 at 20 yrs. 10 m.
DANFORTH, Caroline L. - wife of Levi Danforth,
  1831-1869.
  Clarence E. - 1853-1876.
  John H. - 1865-1890.
WHEELER, Nancy J. Coombs - wife, 1883-1968
  (known as "Jennie").
  Gideon T. - husband, 1876-1953.
  Sarah A. Holbrook - wife, 1879-1902.
  Alice A. - dau, 1898-1918.
  Elmer G. - son, 1906-1907.
  Grace Ella - dau, 1901-1901.
SMALL, James W. - 1837-1909.
  Maria Emeline - wife of James W. Small,
  1846-1933.
  Elvira - dau of James W. & Maria E. Small,
  1881-1903.
  John - father, died 6 Jul 1872 at 84 yrs.
  Nancy - mother, wife of John Small, died 1
  Oct 1872 at 74 yrs. 9 m.
  Ruth - dau of John & Nancy Small, died 21 Jul
  1847 at 25 yrs.
  Mary - dau of John & Nancy Small, died 21 May
  1917 at 90 yrs. 3 m. 15 d.
  John - son of John and Nancy Small, died 25
  Mar 1843 (?) at 7 yrs. (?).
DUNHAM, Mary J. - dau of James & Lucy Dunham,
  died (date not readable) at 22 yrs.
POOL, Hannah - wife of Solomon Pool, died 17 Dec
  1852 at 23 yrs.
DUNHAM, John - died 10 Nov 1854 at 22 yrs. 2 m.
  (Unmarked field stone).
NILES, Hattie F. - dau of John & Rachel Niles,
  died 10 Mar 1856 at 24 yrs. 6 m.

RIDEOUT, Benjamin - died 6 Jun 1862 at 37 yrs.

   Sleep loved husband thy sufferings all are o'er
Pain ne'r again can heave thy breast:
Nor anguish make thy spirit more,
From its eternal guilt rest

   Rebecca H. - wife of Benjamin Rideout, died 19 Dec 1862 at 27 yrs.

   Julia - died 21 Dec 1862 at 9 yrs.) Their
Charles - died 17 Dec 1862 at 6 yrs.) child-
Statira - died 17 Dec 1862 at 15 m.) ren
Wilbur A. - born 20 Apr 1859, died 1 Jul 1904 at 45 yrs. 2 m. 11 d.

SMALL, John B. - died 12 Oct 1846 at 5 yrs.
Sintha A. - died 16 Sep 1846 at 3 yrs.
Children of Isaac P. & Alice Small.
Nathan - son of Isaac P & Alice Small, died 22 Apr 1854 at 14 yrs.
Isaac P. - 17 Sep 1807-25 Feb 1872.
Alice - wife of I. P. Small, 30 May 1808-13 Sep 1889.

RIDEOUT, Rillea E. - dau of Henry & Jane Rideout died 17 Oct 1874 at 19 yrs. 8 m.

SMALL, Olive - wife of Hicks Small, died 24 Jul 1880 at 66 yrs.

MOLOON, Samuel - died 26 Mar 1846 at 73 yrs. 11 m.
Lovey - wife of Samuel Moloon, died 29 Sep 1858 at 78 yrs. 9 m.

MALOON, William - died 31 Aug 1883 at 67 yrs.
Lavina - wife of William Maloon, died 29 Jan 1884 at 74 yrs. 10 m.
James A. - son of William & Lovina Maloon, died 8 Nov 1862 at 12 yrs. 2 m 10 d.
Henrietta - dau of William & Lovina Maloon, died 12 Nov 1862 at 15 yrs. 1 m. 10 d.

Horton — son of William & Lovina Maloon who fell in battle near Shepardstown, Va 16 Jul 1863 at 20 yrs. 5 m. 25 d. — member of Co. G 1st ME Cavalry (GAR marker).

DECOVIN, Marietta — died 2 Oct 1927 at 80 yrs.

SMALL, Eunice — wife of Andrew Small, died 23 Sep 1868 at 79 yrs. 5 m.
  Andrew — died 19 Nov 1844 at 53 yrs. 7 m.

BRIMIGION, Thomas, Mr. — died 17 Dec 1843, at 89 yrs. — A Soldier of the Revolution and a Patriot.
  Ruth, Mrs. — wife of Thomas Brimigion, died 15 Jan 1844 at 76 yrs.
  Eliza — wife of Thomas Brimigion, died 8 Aug 1883 at 73 yrs. (from other sources, Thomas, Jr).

HIGGINS, Hiram — died 14 Mar 1867 at 55 yrs.
  Belinda — died 19 Nov 1891 at 76 yrs.
  Olive — died 5 Aug 1857 at 24 yrs.
  Mary — died 8 Sep 1858 at 17 yrs.
  Alice — died 17 Apr 1859 at 4 yrs.
  Woodbury — 1847-1920.
  James C. — Co E 5th ME Inf, died 3 May 1863 at 22 yrs.

MALOON, Esther M. — 1873-1932.
  Elisha — father, died 15 Feb 1909 at 73 yrs. 5 m. 10 d.
  Margaret S. — mother, wife of Elisha Maloon, died 30 Jan 1918 at 75 yrs. 18 d.
  Statire E. — dau of Elisha & Statire Maloon, died 30 Jan 1863 at 12 yrs. 7 m.

  Loved parents and sisters dear,
  I am not dead but slumber here,
  And brother you I hope to see
  And meet you all in eternity.

  Elisha — died 17 Nov 1866 at 57 yrs. 22 d.

Statire - wife of Elisha Maloon, died 3 Jan 1882 at 69 yrs. 3 m. 9 d.

VICKERY, Rebecca A. - 1844-1923.

THOMAS, Elizabeth B. - 1843-1930.

COX, Delphine A. - died 1 Apr 1879 at 41 yrs.

DAY, Louisa - wife of Isiah Day died 22 Sep 1891 at 75 yrs.

COX, Disier - mother, wife of Isaac Cox, died 12 Nov 1882 at 94 yrs. 28 d.
Isaac - father, died 20 Jul 1860 at 69 yrs. 10 m.

CURTIS, Joseph P. - son of Nehemiah & Jane Curtis, 1843-1904.
Jane - wife of Nehemiah Curtis, died 17 Oct 1852 at 44 yrs. 4 m.
Nehemiah - died 8 Aug 1885 at 77 yrs. 11 m.
Hannah L. - wife of Nehemiah Curtis, 1825-1910.
Isadora M. - wife of George S. Curtis, 1857-1922.

MERRIMAN, Isabella - dau of Robert & Clarissa Merriman, died 3 Dec 1893 at 64 yrs. 21 d.
Sarah J. - sister, dau of R. & C. Merriman, died 1 Feb 1876 at 39 yrs. 10 m.
Clarissa - mother, wife of Robert Merriman, died 15 Feb 1871 at 67 yrs.
Robert - father, died 15 Dec 1869 at 66 yrs.

BATCHELDER, William C. - 1859-1933.
Rosie A. Sampson - his wife, 1864-1930.
Arthur - 1898-1936.
Minerva - dau of Abel E. and Cordelia W. Batchelder, died 1 Sep 1882 at 24 yrs. 11 m. 8 d.
Ruth A. - dau of Abel E. & Cordelia W. Batchelder, died 15 Dec 1866 at 4 yrs. 5 m.
Cordelia W. - mother, wife of Abel E. Batchelder, Esq, died 23 May 1880 at 45 yrs.
Abel E., Esq. - father, died 2 Apr 1912 at 83 yrs. 14 d.

KELLAM, Charles - 1873-1929.
  Mabel H. - his wife, 1874-1945.
ALLEN, Verson L. - 1890-1924.
WOODCOCK, Frank L. - 1869-1932.
  Emma - his wife, 1878-1950.
GREENWOOD, Laura - 1853-1914.
TRICH, Howard - 1904-1926.
LEWIS, Wilbert J. - 1898-1941.
  Byron - 29 Dec 1875-29 Nov 1951.
  Elizabeth H. - 1881-1967.
RIDEOUT, Fred E. - father, 1867-1921.
  Susan J. - mother, his wife, 1868-1940.
PATTERSON, Florence N. - 1887-1946.
  Neal M. - 1882-1945.
MALOON, W. Leslie - father, 1868-1938.
  Maud M. - mother, his wife, 1879-1956.
MITCHELL, Arthur R. - 1896- .
  Ruby M. - his wife, 1896-1922.
HEBB, Ernest F. - 31 Jul 1900-4 May 1948.
  Ina E. - his wife, 28 Jan 1901- .
SMALL, Felix H. - 27 Apr 1903-8 Aug 1973.
  Geneva M. - his wife, 5 Feb 1908-29 Sep 1949.
  Wallace Lincoln - 10 Jan 1865-24 Nov 1950.
  Mary Ann Walsh - his wife, 19 Apr 1863-
  19 Sep 1924.
  Their sons
  Urban C. - 11 Jan 1898-22 Feb 1958.
  Stephen B. - 16 Apr 1891-17 Aug 1972.
RIDEOUT, Lauren N. - 25 Aug 1910-8 Mar 1977.
  Annie C. - his wife, 4 May 1911- .
MARKHAM, Edward, Jr. - 1 Oct 1964-1 Jul 1971.
SMALL, Dorothy L. - 1913-1972.
RIDEOUT, Stanwood G. - 1942-1972.
  Sylvia Poore - 1944-1972.
  Roxanne M. - 1962-1972.
  Connie A. - 1965-1972.
  Stanwood G., Jr. - 1969-1972.

Baby Boy - 1971-1971.
WHEELER, Vivian - 10 Dec 1920-20 Dec 1979.
Ellery - 21 Feb 1910-17 Jun 1982.
HUNTINGTON, Earl A. - 10 May 1882-16 Feb 1972.
Frances Jordan Small - 28 Jan 1893-18 Oct 1985.
GOULD, John H. - 1896-1965.
Hulday A. Parker - 1905-1985.
John M. - 1926-1955.
Marie J. - wife, 25 Feb 1957-2 May 1981.
BYRNE, John K. - 1860-1924.
Miriam - his wife, 1863-1944.
WAGG, James - husband, 27 Aug 1889-3 Nov 1933.
Edna L. - wife of, 1897-1982.
Their son - inf, 1929-1929.
Merton E. - 1921-   .
Beatrice H. - his wife, 1930-
Lorraine - 1958-1958.)
Ralph - 1962-1962.   ) Infants
ANDERSON, Maynard P. - 1922-   .
Virginia R. - 1924-   .
HOLBROOK, Isaac H. - 1865-1941.
Georgia M. - 1869-1928.
Ruth L. - 10 Jun 1913-7 Aug 1980.
MERRILL, Leon R. -1888-1940.
Angie E. - 1899-19   .
Ethel Mavis - 2 May 1927-23 Jun 1963.
She was "Wife & Mother of 8 Children."
GODDARD, Warren E. - Maine Pvt 151 Depot Brigade World War I, 9 Oct 1896-17 Dec 1970 (another stone 9 Oct 1895).
Lillian R. Tuttle - his wife, 3 Oct 1883-1 Oct 1963.
CURTIS, Linwood L. - 9 Sep 1871-27 Oct 1930.
Children
Eughenia L. - 12 Dec 1914-5 Jun 1915.
Albert H. - 15 Sep 1913-31 Jul 1936.

SMALL, Margaret Tuttle - 10 Nov 1832-25 Dec 1924.
MORGAN, Carliss N. - 1911-   .
STARBIRD, Beatrice M. - 1910-1982.
WHITTAKER, Vesta R. - 1902-   .
CURTIS, Edren - ME Pvt U. S. Army World War II,
  6 Mar 1905-7 Dec 1973.
  Elmer L. - 1903-1979.
  Gabrielle J. - 1907-   .
LAVALLEE, Adelia - 1897-   .
COULOMBE, Adelard - 1894-   .
BROWN, Ethel M. - 15 May 1886-2 Jan 1957.
  Joseph V. - 2 Aug 1888-14 Oct 1963 (Auburn
  Police Dept marker).
MINOTT, Rufus R. - died in Havana 8 Jun 1858
  at 28 yrs. 2 m.
  Thomas S. - died 27 Aug 1883 at 87 yrs. 2 m.
  Fanny G. - his wife, 1801-1888.
  (There are two Minott stones which are not
  readable.)
  Josie - (head stone not readable).
BROWN, Harriet - mother, wife of Capt Joseph
  Brown, died 25 Jul 1878 at 38 yrs. 4 m. 8 d.

  She lived and died in hope of eternal life.

  Joseph F., Capt. - 1835-1906.
  Elizabeth C. - his wife, 1845-1939.
  Frances M. - dau of Joseph F. & Elizabeth
  C. Brown, 1881-1913.
MORRISON, George R. - 1834-1915.
  Marietta S. Minott - his wife, 1841-1932.
  Nancy A. - wife of Geo. R. Morrison, died
  26 Apr 1862 at 33 yrs. 7 m.
ALLEN, Royce W. - ME Pvt 42 Inf 12 Div World
  War I, 6 Feb 1893-5 Feb 1946.
DARLING, Laura J. - mother, 1866-1948.
  Charles R. - father, 1856-1935.
SMALL, Viola A. - 1862-1866.

   Ella B. - 1874-1877.
   Frank B. - 1866-1888.
   Children of Lewis & Annie F. Small
   Lewis - 1836-1897.
   Annie F. - wife, 1836-1896.
CARVER, Willbert S. - 1857-1931.
   Isabella - 1855-1927.
   Mary A. - 1831-1916.
SNELL, Asa - 1815-1891.
   Amy Greenleaf - his wife, 1830-1892.
   Elfrida A. - dau Asa & Amy Snell, died (not readable) 1862 at 9 yrs. 2 m.
   Laura A. - dau of Asa & Amy Snell, died 13 Aug 1862 at 13 yrs. (?).
   Emmer J. - dau Asa & Amy Snell, died (not readable) 1862 at 10 yrs. (not readable).
   Joseph W. - (next to Emmer - not readable).
SMALL, Nathaniel - 2 Jul 1818-3 May 1882.
   Elizabeth P. - his wife, 9 Oct 1827-4 Feb 1890.
   Their Children
   Emily - 4 Oct 1848-18 Mar 1850.
   Alfred E. - 6 Aug 1872-16 Feb 1890.
PRESTON, Margery A. - their dau, 27 Dec 1850-14 Apr 1899.
   Frank A. - her son, 28 Oct 1883-11 Oct 1899.
GROVER, Abel T. - 27 May 1820-11 Jan 1901.
   Sarah Roberts - his wife, 15 Jan 1824-4 Dec 1901.
   Abel T., Jr. - 7 Jul 1867-27 Jul 1951.
   Tinnie May Nowell - his wife, 27 Jan 1881-22 Aug 1906.
ALLEN, George L. - father, 1855-1933.
   Hattie M. - mother, his wife, 1862-1943.
   Weston R. - 1891-1967.
TOWNSEND, Frank B. - 7 Jun 1863-31 Mar 1915.

ROBERTS, Susie T. - 1 May 1866-15 Mar 1943
  (nee Townsend - DAR marker).
COX, Joseph H. - 1869-1929.
  Rachel Townsend - his wife, 1887-1966.
CROSS, Russell N. - ME Sgt 238 PW Escort Co,
  World War I, 20 Jul 1894-26 Dec 1952.
RANKS, Thomas - father, 1855-1939.
  Nellie E. - mother, his wife, 1854-1930.
RIDEOUT, Wilber A. - 1859-1904.
  Sadie - his wife, 1859-1950.
  Lester F. - 1882-1957.
  Winifred - 1889-1969 (funeral home marker).
  Henry E. - 1883-1959 (funeral home marker).
SMALL, John - 1862-1952.
  Laura E. - his wife, 1864-1935 (DAR marker).
  Their children
  Ethel W. - 1894-1914.
  John Raymond - 1896-1915.
  Milton H. - 1899-1989.
  Alice L. Wilson - his wife, 1903-   .
RIDEOUT, Lena E. - mother, wife of Wm, 27 Sep
  1888-3 Mar 1956.

  Just when life was sweetest and you could
  have lived your best,
  The gates of heaven opened and God took
  you home to rest.
  In our hearts your memory lingers sweetly,
  tender, kind and true.
  There is not a day, dear Mother, that we
  do not think of you.

            My Darling Mother
  Someone I love, I know loves me.
  Mother, of mine, true as can be.
  Ever I think of the happy days flown,
  Remembering you always dear Mother.
                        Dorothy

  Viola - (a small old marble stone with nothing on it except the name).
  Addie Martin - 1919-1945.
  Alice Stover - 1917-1936.
COOMBS, Marcia C. - 1847-1927.
HARKNESS, Ralph Thomas - 1923-1948.
  S. May Rideout - his wife, 1929-1950.

     My Darling Sister
  Someone I love, I know loves me.
  Sister of mine, true as can be.
  Ever I think of the happy days flown,
  Remembering you always Sister, my own.

RIDEOUT, Robert L. - 1891-1970.
  George M. - 1922-1959.
MALOY, Margaret L. - 1946-1979.
ALLISON, Louise - 1883-1959.
HALL, Harry - 1895-1974.
ROBERTS, Mary E. - his wife, born 10 Dec 1843, died 1 Mar 1907.
  Eliza J. - wife of N. Roberts, born 26 Feb 1832, died 28 Jun 1887.
  Nath. - born 11 Jun 1830, died 4 Feb 1915.
  Etta - born 2 Feb 1867, died 11 Feb 1867.
SAMPSON, Giles L. -) No individual dates
 Lizzie M. -   ) but 1904 on top of
 Annie F. -   ) monument
  Rosalinda A. - dau of Findley & Roxana K. Sampson, died 10 Feb 1864 at 19 yrs. 6 m.
  Roxana K. - mother, wife of Findley Sampson, died 14 Apr 1883 at 70 yrs. 10 m. 3 d.
  Findley - father, died 1 Apr 1890 at 76 yrs.
MARR, Edward - 18 Aug 1839-24 Dec 1891 (GAR marker).
  Fannie E. Healy - wife of E. Marr, 8 Apr 1840-12 Dec 1904.
  Winifred F. - dau, 1872-1955.

COOMBS, Zebulon - A volunteer in the War of 1812 (b. 20 Mar 1780), died 12 Apr 1850.
  Nancy - his wife, The first white female child born in the town of Bowdoin, born 4 Feb 1779, died 14 Dec 1863.
  Abner C. - 1851-1932.
  Abbie B. - his wife, 1850-1933.
ELWELL, Helena F. Coombs - 1903-1940.
COOMBS, Luella - dau of John & Betsey Coombs, born 20 Jan 1850, died 14 Jul 1867.
  Ada - wife of John Coombs, 21 Jun 1897-22 Nov 1947.
  John - born 8 Jan 1810, died 7 Dec 1897.
  Betsey - his wife, born 10 Oct 1811, died 21 Sep 1896.
  Dennis D. - husband, born 3 Oct 1820, died 4 Sep 1887.
  Lavina Carr - wife of Dennis D. Coombs, born 16 Aug 1818, died 14 Sep 1903.
ALLEN, Joel S. - son of C. H. & I. E. Allen, 1886-1890.
  Joel S. - son of C. H. & C. D. Allen, 1906-1907.
CARD, Joel - died 4 Jun 1840 at 84 yrs.
  William, Maj. - died 1 Jun 1868 at 64 yrs. 5 m.
  Contentment - wife of William Card, born 28 Jun 1801, died 24 Feb 1883 at 81 yrs. 2 m. 27 d.
  William, Jr. - d. 29 Nov 1864 at 32 yrs. 10 m. 14 d.
ALLEN, Charles H. - 1864-1933.
  Clara D. - wife of C. H. Allen, 1881-1967.
  Ida E. - wife of C. H. Allen, 1867-1899.
DEGOVIN, Hattie F. - mother, wife of John Degovin, died 29 Apr 1886 at 29 yrs. 11 m.
HOLBROOK, Isaac - died 8 Apr 1886 at 71 yrs. 10 m.

Harriet - mother, his wife, died 18 Apr 1892 at 75 yrs. 10 m.
APPLEBY, Sarah - wife of Joseph Appleby, died 8 Jan 1874 at 91 yrs.
Joseph - died 29 Dec 1834 at 50 yrs.
GROVER, George W. - died 9 Mar 1886 at 30 yrs. 11 m.
(There is a foot stone marked P. S.)
SMALL, Joshua - died 10 Mar 1835 at 61 yrs. 2 m.
ALLEN, Joel S. - 1840-1915.
Statira - 1841-1922.
CARD, Ella M. - dau of B. W. & F. R. Card, died 19 Nov 1867 at 3 m. 7 d.
(There is a slate stone which is not readable.)
Benjamin W. - 1833-1903.
Frances R. - his wife, 1834-1914.
Nellie May - 1868-1868.
Carrie - wife of B. F. Card, 10 Mar 1870-27 Aug 1892.
Leroy - son of John & Emily Card, 1896-1896.
GILLESPIE, Joseph - died 19 Dec 1874 at 66 yrs. 9 m.
Martha Blood - died 15 Aug 1872 at 76 yrs. 3 m.
(The stones for Joseph and Martha are identical and next to each other, but the name Gillespie is not on Martha's stone; it is assumed that Martha was the wife of Joseph Gillespie, however.)
BLOOD, Martha - died 15 Aug 1872 at 76 yrs. 3 m.
GILLESPIE, John - died 12 Jun 1837 at 75 yrs.
Jane - his wife, died 31 Dec 1857 at 87 yrs.
GROVER, James A. - 18 Mar 1848-11 Feb 1932
(Masonic emblem).
BISHOP, Josephine A. - 9 Apr 1849-7 Dec 1897.
BRANCH, Nellie A. - 1845-1923.
APPLEBY, Nathaniel S. - 2 Mar 1810-24 Mar 1883.
Rachel E. Temple - his wife, 9 Nov 1814-31 May 1886.

Abbie A. - 6 Feb 1843-22 Sep 1894.
Hannah - dau of Joseph & Sarah Appleby, died 14 Nov 1863 at 49 yrs.
Alden - son of Joseph & Sarah Appleby, died 5 Feb 1854 at 26 yrs. 7 d.
Abigail - died 28 Jan 1831 at 14 yrs. 8 m.
Levi - died in Peru, ILL 20 Dec 1839 at 27 yrs.
Children of Joseph & Sarah Appleby
Levi - 3rd ME Vol 61-62, 29th Co. Mass. Art. 64-65, 1840-1919.

GROVER, Mary A. - his wife, 13 Mar 1860-3 Jul 1901 (last name not clear but verified by ref to Bowdoin Town Report for Year Ending 22 Feb 1902).
Ezekiel A. - 24 Mar 1824-7 Nov 1902.
Maria E. Cox - his wife, 20 Apr 1828-26 Mar 1915.

BAILEY, Perley T. - 1890-1937 (Masonic emblem).
Emma M. - his wife, 1886-
Gerald E. - 1917-1917.

ALLEN, Raymond Charles - 2 Jul 1910-18 Dec 1984 (on front of monument Born here 1910 Died here 1984).
Vera Wagg - his wife, 23 Aug 1924

WHEELER, Ervin - son, 1912-1987 (this grave is on the lot of Gideon T. Wheeler, p. 65).

DENNISON, Laurence E. - 2 Oct 1939-15 Jun 1985.

WHITE, John F. - CM3, U. S. Navy, World War II, 13 Apr 1925-28 Oct 1985.
Ruby R. - 1925-

North Cemetery - at the intersection of Routes 201 and 125 in Bowdoin, go towards Lisbon Falls. Turn right at Bowdoin Center. Go 4.8 miles. The cemetery is on the left. At one time there was a church next to the cemetery called the North Church.

When we copied these inscriptions in 1972, the cemetery was in a deplorable condition. An article (written in 1913) cited the condition of the North Cemetery as a disgrace to the memory of the Revolutionary Patriots resting there. The Bowdoin Historical Society took over the care of the cemetery in 1972, and the local Boy Scouts have maintained the cemetery since 1990.

Fortunately in 1931-32 the inscriptions were copied for inclusion in the DAR Historical and Genealogical Collections. Information from the inscriptions were incorporated into the Vital Records of Bowdoin, Maine, edited by Rachel Townsend Cox and published in three volumes in 1945. By referring to these sources we have been able to include information no longer available.

However, even with care of the cemetery since 1972, stones have disappeared or deteriorated beyond legibility, and without a doubt this was true even when inscriptions were first copied. It is also highly probable that through the years fallen stones have been stood up in other than the original locations.

LYDSTROM, Lizzie - Earth life closed in Auburn, Me. 16 Sep 1869 at 26 yrs. 5 m. 15 d.

This stone has been stolen in recent years and

has not been recovered. At the top of the stone there was an indented circle with a hand holding a ribbon like piece on which is written "To My Earth Friends." Below the circle is the following:

   This is to tell you I still live.
   In mansions of the Spirit world.
   There is No Death -- this truth believe.
   O, 'tis a greater wealth than gold.
   Nor have I gone far off -- above --
   My heaven home's with those I love:

   Tis Lizzie's thought in Spirit Sphere.
   These words impressed as written here.

             Yours affectionately
             In Spirit Love and Live

                    LIZZIE

GROVER, Happy - wife of Isaac Grover, died 26 Nov 1862 at 50 yrs. 9 m.
  Isaac - died 19 Nov 1859 at 57 yrs. 1 m.
VARNUM, Marilla A. - dau of Ralph & Saloma Varnum, died 23 Dec 1865 at 24 yrs. 10 m.

   A few days of sorrow, a few days of pain
   A few fiery trials and victories to gain
   Oh then we shall meet our loved ones on that
     shore
   Where all who love Jesus will live evermore.

  Ralph - died 19 Feb 1885 at 68 yrs. 7 m.
  Saloma - wife of Ralph Varnum, died 29 Jul 1873 at 59 yrs. 10 m.
FOSTER, B. W. - died 20 Jun 1873 at 35 yrs. 4 m.
  Mary A. - dau of B. W. & Alice Foster, died 4 May 1873 at 9 m.

RANKS, Charlie W. - son of C. F. & L. B. Ranks, died 19 Aug 1873 at 7 m.
  Annie Ridley - wife of John Ranks, born 26 Feb 1818, died 9 Nov 1905 at 87 yrs.
  John - born 14 Feb 1776, died 28 May 1867, at 91 yrs.

CARVILL, Anna Dennett - 26 Oct 1818-18 Mar 1879.

DENNETT, Susannah - wife of Moses Dennett, Esq, died 4 May 1853 at 68 yrs. 10 m.
  Moses - died 6 Nov 1846 at 74 yrs. 8 m.

BRIRY, Mary S. - wife of Joseph Briry, Esq, died 23 Jun 1889 at 95 yrs. 6 m.
  Joseph, Esq. - died 26 Jan 1843 at 50 yrs.

DENNETT, Anna - wife of John Dennett, died 1 Mar 1866 at 79 yrs.
  John - died (stone is broken but Town Records show he was born 1767 and bur. 27 Nov 1843; DAR records agree).

BATCHELDER, Ruth - wife of Samuel E. Batchelder, died 1 Aug 1877 at 89 yrs.
  Samuel E. - died 8 Nov 1863 at 82 yrs. 8 m. 13 d.
  Sarah, Miss - dau of Saml. & Ruth Batchelder died 21 Jan. (21 not clear and year unreadable but DAR records show 24 Jan 1843 at 19 y. See also Vol II, p. 33 <u>Bowdoin</u> <u>Vital</u> <u>Records</u>.)

STARBIRD, Margaret - died 6 Oct 1831 at 24 yrs.
  James - died 26 Jan 1839 at 30 yrs.

  Come see the end of man
  For you must surely go
  Your life is nothing but a span
  Like all things here below.

DENNETT, Wm. H. Harrison - son of Nathl. & Mary Dennett, died 6 May 1842 at 18 m.
  Marshall - son of Nathl. & Mary B. Dennett, died 17 Jun 1848 at 4 yrs. 6 m.

CHASE, Emily - wife of Orrin B. Chase, died 5 Mar 1879 at 57 yrs. 2 m.

   Home is not here mother is not
   Dark is her room empty her chair
   Angels have taken her out from our care
   And lifted her over life's storm

Oren B. - died 9 Aug 1860 at 43 yrs.
STARBIRD, Isaac - died 7 Sep 1883 at 72 yrs. 10 m. 17 d.
Sarah H. - wife of Isaac Starbird, died 21 Mar 1863 at 49 yrs. 7 m. 24 d.
VERNEY, Wm. - died ? Mar 1857.
GROVER, Eleanor R. - dau of Andrew and Ann Grover, died 29 Oct 1843 at 19 yrs. 6 m.
Mehitable J. - died 19 Jun 1849 at 23 yrs. 6 m.
Ann, Mrs. - wife of Andrew Grover, died 28 May 1836 at 39 yrs. 6 m.
Andrew - died 26 Jul 1868 at 71 yrs. 7 m.
Mehitable, Mrs. - wife of Mr. Andrew Grover, who died 26 Nov 1831 at 59 yrs. 7 d.
(It appears that this stone has been reset and in doing so the price of the stone, $8.25, now shows.)
HIGGINS, Mehitabel, Mrs. - wife of Capt Jeremiah Higgins, who died 5 Mar 1842 at 55 yrs.
THURLOW, Jacob, Mr. - of Charlestown, Mass, who died 5 Oct 1832 at 38 yrs.

   I've left my wife and children dear
   My body in the dust has fell
   When the last trumpet I shall hear
   I'll rise and with my Saviur dwell.

HAMSCOM, Samuel - died 24 Aug 1851 at 73 yrs. 3 m.
TARR, Joanna - dau of Joseph, Jr. & Lydia Tarr, died 14 Sep 1851 at 17 yrs. 4 m.
  Joseph, Jr. - died 31 Jul 1851 at 49 yrs.
GROVER, Hannah - wife of Jonathan, died 17 Oct 1863 at 81 yrs.
  Jonathan - who died 27 Jun 1822 at 49 yrs. (the "9" is backwards).
HANSCOM, Jerusha - died 19 Jun 1830 at 84 yrs.
PRATT, John, Mr. - died 8 Dec 1818 at 51 yrs.
JELISON, Nathaniel, Mr. - (the "r" is above the "M") - who died 3 Dec 1804 at 54 yrs.

The body here intombed in dust,
The soul rejoining with the dust
Ye Saints rejoi<u>s</u>e before the throne
Dear friends his loss you all will mourn.

STARBIRD, Saml. - died 1 Sep 1839 at 81 yrs.
  Alicia - died 24 Mar 1840 at 82 yrs.
LYDSTON, Hannah - died 4 Sep 1833 at 1 yr. 8 m.
  Jessie H. - died 7 Jul 1846 at 9 yrs. 4 m.
  Children of Timothy & Didamia Lydston.
  Timothy, Dea. - died 30 Jul 1875 at 81 yrs. 9 m. 19 d.
  Didamia - wife of Timothy Lydston, died 1 Aug 1854 at 53 yrs. 3 m. 20 d.
  Ellen D. - died 8 Apr 1859 at 18 yrs. 7 m. 21 d (reads Daughter<u>s</u> of Timothy & Mary Lydston).
DUNLAP, David, Mr. - who died 17 Jun 1833 at 60 yrs.

I from corruption soon shall rise
By virtue of my Saviours blood
To live and reign above the skies
With Christ my Saviour and my God

ALLEN, Eleanor B. - dau of Rufus & Mahitable Allen, died 7 Sep 1848 at 17 yrs. 4 m.
Rufus, Capt. - died 24 Apr 1871 at 69 yrs. 1 m.
Daniel - died 4 Oct 1840 at 81 yrs.
Margery, Mrs. - died 29 Dec 1842 at 77 yrs.
LYDSTON, Roby, Mr. - died 7 Nov 1835 at 48 yrs.
William - died 4 Aug 1835 at 81 yrs.
Sarah - died 3 Nov 1835 at 76 yrs.
GROVER, Lydia, Mrs. - wife of Mr. David Grover, who died 9 Feb 1835 at 38 yrs. 10 m.
(There are footstones with "J. T." and "E. T.")
CHASE, Elizabeth B. - dau of Jas. & Mehetabel Chase, died 4 Sep 1827 at 5 yrs.
GROVER, Jordan N. - died 18 Nov 1843 at 30 yrs.
HIGGINS, Zaccheus - died 14 Mar 1848 at 76 yrs. 3 m.
GROVER, Margareta, Miss - only dau of Mr. Israel & Mrs. Margaret Grover, died 17 Sep 1830 at 20 yrs. (DAR and Vital Records, 30 yrs).
CHASE, Isaac, Mr. - died 6 Feb 1842 at 82 yrs. (Selectmen's records show him born 1760).
Elizabeth B. - wife, died 4 Sep 1827 at 50 yrs. (stone now gone but data in Vital Records, Vol. II).
OLIVER, Mary - wife of John Oliver, died 14 Apr 1844 at 75 yrs.
John - died 21 Sep 1848 at 80 yrs.
MAXWELL, William H. - son of William & Charity Maxwell, died 5 Dec 1855 at 2 yrs. 3 m.
STARBIRD, Addie A. - dau of Rufus S. & C. S. Starbird, died 15 Sep 1867 at 18 yrs. 2 m.
RIGGS, Sarah Jane - dau of Enoch & Nancy Riggs, died 1 Jan 1846 at 19 yrs.
DUNLAP, Lucy Jane - dau of Eben & Sarah Dunlap, died 15 May 1844 at 11 m.
Eben - died 26 Jul 1849 at 40 yrs. 9 m.

STARBIRD, Moses - died 19 Jul 1854 at 73 yrs. 10 m.
Lucy - died 21 Dec 1873 at 89 yrs.
(The dates and ages were not readable when we copied and have been taken from the Vital Records, Vol. II, p. 122.)
CHASE, Bunker - died 13 Jun 1863 at 57 yrs. 7 m.
Ann - wife of Bunker Chase, born 11 May 1806, died 24 Feb 1884 (dates not readable now, so taken from DAR list and Vol II, p. 45 Vital Records).
James - died 25 Nov 1852 at 70 yrs.
RIDLEY, Mary - wife of William Ridley, died 23 Oct 1875 at 85 yrs. 6 m. 24 d.

Blessed are the dead who die in the Lord.

William - died 14 Oct 1860 at 77 yrs. 8 m.

FARNUM, J. Franklin - son of Thomas & Lucy A. Farnum, died 26 Aug 1853 at 11 yrs. 11 m. 1 d.
NORTON, Noah, Rev. - died 6 Jan 1851 at 62 Yrs. (age from DAR list and Vol. II, p. 95, Vital Records).
Sally - wife of Noah Norton, died 29 Mar 1857 at 68 yrs. 5 m.
RIDLEY, Elisha P. - son of Alexander & Jane Ridley, died 5 May 1872 at 15 yrs. 1 m. 15 d.
Rachel J. Aderton - mother, wife of Alexander Ridley, 27 May 1833-15 Mar 1908.
Alexander - father, 24 Jun 1827-18 Jan 1916.
ELWELL, John S. - died 6 Jun 1879 at 79 yrs. 1 m. 14 d. (The DAR list shows age as 77 yrs; however, 1850 Census for Bowdoin shows he was 50 then.)
Margery - widow of John S. Elwell and former

wife of Roby Lydston, died 24 Oct 1881 at 82 yrs. 3 m.
Jennie A. - wife of John L. Elwell, died 24 Feb 1877 at 29 yrs. 9 m. 14 d.
LYDSTON, Minnie - born in Murphy's Camp, Cal, 2 Oct 1864, died in Chicago, Ill, 22 Feb 1868.
Roby, born in Lewiston, ME 11 Mar 1866, died in Chicago, Ill 16 Feb 1868.
Children of G. N. & Lucy A. Lydston
RIDLEY, Willie A. - son of Alex. & Rachel J. Ridley, died 21 Mar 1864 at 1 yr. 4 m. 7 d.

Sleep on dear Willie
And take thy rest
God called thee home
He thought it best.

ALEXANDER, Robert E. - son of Robert & Sarah Alexander, died 4 Jun 1849 at 10 m.
Elizabeth - wife of Robert Alexander, died 12 Feb 1849 at 81 yrs.
Robert - died 6 Sep 1849 at 83 yrs.
Timothy - died 25 Jul 1855 at 27 yrs. 10 m.
LYDSTON, Harriet A. - wife of William Lydston, died 16 Mar 1855 at 26 yrs. 10 m.
William J. - died 31 Jan 1853 at 9 d.
Helen M. - died 15 May 1853 at 3 yrs. 1 m. 15 d.
Children of William & Harriet A. Lydston

These tender buds, so young, so fair,
Called home by early doom.
Just came to show what lovely flowers
In Paradise will bloom.

Margery - dau of G. N. & Lucy A. Lydston, died 6 Jun 1875 at 9 m. 5 d. in Chicago.

The following inscriptions are on the DAR list but were not found by us in North Cemetery:

ADAMS, Susan, Mrs. - died 1 Mar 1868 at 58 yrs.
BERRY, Joseph - died 26 Jan 1843 at 50 yrs.
   Mary S. - wife of Joseph Berry, died 23 Jun 1889 at 95 yrs.
CHASE, Mehitable - died 23 Mar 1860.
   Laura E. - died 15 Sep 1848 at 3 yrs.
LYDSTON, Ellen - died 8 Apr 1859 at 20 m. 10 d.
   Lizzie M. - died 4 Apr 1879 at 18 yrs. 7 m.
STARBIRD, Sarah - died 21 Mar 1863 at 49 yrs. 7 m.
   Moses - died 21 Jul 1854 at 26 yrs.
TARR, Joseph - died 5 Jan 1845 at 87 yrs.
   Debora - wife of Joseph Tarr, died 1835 at 75 yrs.

Millay Cemetery - at intersection of Routes 201 and 125 in Bowdoin, go 2.3 miles on Route 201 towards Richmond. Turn right on a woods road and go approximately 3/4ths-1 mile. You will pass a house or hunting lodge on the right. Shortly after this building, turn left. Cemetery will be on the right. These inscriptions were copied in 1973.

LANCASTER, George C. - father, 1857-1932.
  Mary A. Stinson - mother, his wife, 1861-1908.
RINES, Bernice - 13 Jul 1923-7 Jul 1925.
  Geraldine - dau of Albert H. and Ethel M. Rines, 9 May 1915-19 Jul 1915.
POTTER, Henry R. - 10 Nov 1841-4 Jun 1908.
  Cornelia G. - wife of Henry R. Potter, 29 Jul 1841 (no date of death).
LANCASTER, Charles C. - father, died 19 Apr 1911 at 78 yrs. 8 m.
  Abbie M. - mother, wife of Charles C. Lancaster, died 14 Aug 1844 at 48 yrs.
  Frances E. - wife of C. C. Lancaster, died 8 Mar 1904 at 73 yrs.
JONES, Abbie F. - 1814-1901.
HUNTINGTON, Henry E. - died 22 Dec 1893 at 43 yrs. 6 m.
POTTER, Webb H. - 6 Jan 1868-3 May 1890.
GETCHELL, Aaron - father, died 2 Jun 1878 at 78 yrs.
  Adah - mother, wife of Aaron Getchell, died 16 Mar 1889 at 81 yrs. 10 m.
  Aletice - dau of Aaron and Adah Getchell, died 12 Jan 1858 at 13 yrs. 15 d.
  Vesta M. - dau of Aaron & Adah Getchell, 26 Feb 1853-12 May 1920.
  Charles F. - 8 Jan 1843-2 Jul 1906.

Allie A. Lord - his wife, 10 May 1849-23 Apr 1938.
VARNEY, Zacheus - Company F, 24th ME Vols, 1830-1909.
Charlotte Williams - his wife, 1832-1863.
Martha A. - their dau, 1856-1862.
Martha Armstrong - dau of Zacheus & Charlotte Varney, died 19 Jan 1862 at 5 yrs. 8 m.

She died to sin: she died to care:
But for a moment felt the rod
Then, rising on the viewless air
Spread her light wings and soared to God.

GRAVES, Mary J. - 1845-1939.
RANDALL, Helen E. - 1843-1931.
ADAMS, Sarah, Mrs. - died 4 Mar 1864 at 73 yrs. 6 m.

We mourn thy loss dear mother
We miss thy smiling face
And feel that earth without thee
Is but a desert place.

RANDALL, Elizabeth A. - 1820-1912.
CURTIS, Luther - father, died 20 Feb 1887 at 76 yrs. 7 m. 7 d.
Mary - mother, wife of Luther Curtis, died 9 Apr 1888 at 78 yrs. 10 m. 23 d.
Mary E. - dau of Luther & Mary Curtis, died 10 Nov 1861 at 17 yrs.
Charles - son of Luther & Mary Curtis died 19 Nov 1861 at 13 yrs. 6 m.
Our Baby - no dates.
Harry M. - son of Frank & Maria Curtis, died 15 Apr 1884 at 1 yr. 8 m.
VARNEY, Charles H. - son of H. S. & Eliza Varney died 19 Sep 1862 at 7 m. 19 d.

Eliza M. - wife of Humphrey S. Varney, 1833-1918.
Humphrey S. - died 10 Oct 1891 at 66 yrs.
Hiram, Jr. - son of Hiram & Thankful Varney, died in Washington, DC, 16 Jun 1862 at 22 yrs. 6 m. 27 d, Member of Company C 32d Mass. Regt.
Hiram - died 7 Sep 1881 at 81 yrs. 9 m.
Thankful - wife of Hiram, died 2 Dec 1855 at 55 yrs. (This stone was broken and only Dec 1855 readable. However, p. 127, <u>Death Records</u> of Bowdoinham, Maine compiled by Doris M. Rowland, 1967, shows complete information. Mrs. Rowland included a few Bowdoin inscriptions in her book.)

GOVE, Elijah - died 8 Dec 1889 at 57 yrs.

CURTIS, Henry M. - died 31 Dec 1862 at 28 yrs. 7 m. 9 d (Masonic emblem and Civil War marker).

GRAVES, Katherine J. - mother, died 4 Jun 1898 at 75 yrs. 11 m.
Our Babe - died 16 Apr 1862.

BICKMORE, Henrietta M. - wife of C. S. Bickmore, 1863-1895.

POTTER, Elvira A. - wife of Waitstill Potter, died 12 Dec 1879 at 65 yrs. 9 m. 27 d.
Waitstill - died 7 May 1885 at 82 yrs.
Isabel - wife of Waitstill Potter, died 10 Feb 1855 at 49 yrs. 10 m.

WILLIAMS, Isabel C. - dau of Daniel & Martha Williams, died 6 Jan 1865 at 8 yrs. 5 m.
Daniel A. - died 30 Jan 1878 at 60 yrs. 8 m 15 d.

PAINE, Lucretia - wife of Simeon Paine, died 3 Nov 1880 at 72 yrs.

WILLIAMS, Mary E. - wife of Moses Williams, died 14 Nov 1900 at 76 yrs. 10 m.
Dennis C. - son of Moses & Hannah Williams, died 26 Mar 1853 at 1 yr.

Isaac C. – son of Moses & Hannah Williams, died 1 Jan 1837.
William C. – son of Moses & Hannah Williams, died 26 Mar 1852 at 10 yrs. 8 m.
George – son of Moses & Hannah Williams, died 24 Nov 1811 at 2 yrs. 5 m.
Child (prob.) – died 1831 at 1 yr. (broken stone).
Hannah – wife of Moses Williams, died 8 May 1860 at 47 yrs. 4 d.
Moses – father, died 6 Aug 1882 at 73 yrs.
George – died 22 Jul 1856 at 77 yrs.
Grace – his wife, died 3 Apr 1842 (age underground).

BARNES, Abigail – wife of Elbridge G. Barnes, died 5 May 1818 at 33 yrs. 5 m.
John – died 24 May 1842 at 74 yrs.
Mary, Mrs. – wife of John Barnes, died 15 Sep 1833 at 52 yrs.

PATTERSON, Joseph R., Jr. – son of Joseph R. and Eliza J. Patterson, died 2 Jan 1863 at 18 yrs. 8 m, A Member of Co A 19th Maine Regm't.
Eliza P. – dau of Joseph R. & Eliza J. Patterson, died 27 Mar 1861 at 14 yrs. 11 m.
Eliza J. – wife of Joseph R. Patterson, died 21 Jun 1856 at 34 yrs. 5 m.

CURTIS, Betsey – wife of Charles Curtis, died 13 Aug 1874 at 84 yrs. 9 m.
Charles – died 10 Apr 1850 at 77 yrs. 4 m.
Lydia, Mrs. – died 18 Apr 1831 at 85 yrs. – relict of Charles Curtis of Woolwich.

BLANCHARD – Remember, died 23 Apr 1806 at 17 d.
I. C. – 1820 (small field stone with just "I.C.B.").
(1 small unmarked stone).
Isaiah C., Mr. – died 5 Sep 1820 (Mrs. Rowland (ref. previous) shows age 22).

MILLAY, Ellen – died 15 Aug 1864 at 70 yrs. 9 m.

Rebecca – dau of James & Eunice Millay, died 30 Apr 1843 at 22 m. 14 d.
James K. – died 23 Mar 1893 at 79 yrs. 2 m.
Eunice – his wife, died 28 Aug 1889 at 75 yrs.
Ellen – died 15 Aug 1864 at 70 yrs. 9 m.
Rebecca – dau of J. K. & Eunice Millay died 30 Aug 1843 at 1 yr. 10 m.
James H. – 1848-1930.
Martha E. Purinton – his wife, 1853-1931.

BATES, Mary – wife of Alexander, died 12 Sep 1848 (Sep from Rowland ref previously).

GOVE, Abbie E. – wife of Elijah Gove, died 21 Sep 1882 at 54 yrs. 10 m. 21 d.

RIDLEY, Martha S. – wife of George Ridley, died 6 Feb 1881 at 76 yrs. 5 m. 5 d.
George – died 7 Oct 1851 at 61 yrs. 4 m.
_____ (perhaps Ridley) – died 29 Nov 1824 at 29 yrs 6 m. (broken stone).

DAVIS, James – died 26 Jun 1870 at 74 yrs.
Charlotte – wife of James Davis, died 21 Dec 1870 at 67 yrs. 12 m.

WILLIAMS – Lydia – 2nd wife of Jonathan Williams, died 27 Nov 1881 at 76 yrs. 11 m.
Jonathan – died 29 Jan 1865 at 64 yrs.
Sarah, Mrs. – wife of Jonathan Williams, died 24 Mar 1829 at 34 yrs.
Our baby – died 6 Apr 1890 at 3 wks.
Gertrude M. – dau of Henry A. & Gertrude A. Williams, died 30 Sep 1888 at 3 m.
Ralph H. – son of Henry H. & Gertrude A. Williams, died 28 Aug 1907 at 11 yrs.

MILLAY, Horace J. – 3 Jan 1890-13 Jan 1954.
Bertha E. – his wife, 21 May 1887-

BLANCHARD – Diana – mother, wife of Loyel Blanchard, died 5 Jan 1898 at 75 yrs. 5 m. 24 d.
Loyel – father, died 9 May 1883 at 73 yrs. 8 m.
Benj., Mr. – died 10 Jun 1821 at 48 yrs.

Deborah, Mrs. - wife of Benj. Blanchard,
died 22 Dec 1842 at 77 yrs.
WHEELER, George - 1835-1907.
Annie M. Hunt - his wife, 1839-1910.
REED, James T.-husband of Melvina A. Adams,
1880-1963.
Melvina A. Adams - wife of James T. Reed,
1875-1925.

My lamps are trimmed and burning bright.

(There are two fallen stones which we could
not lift to read.)

PATTEN, Etta F. - wife of Orator Patten, 14 Feb
1856-9 May 1909.
BAKER, Abbie F. - wife of William B. Baker,
died 19 Feb 1908 at 60 yrs. 2 m. 26 d.
William - husband Abbie F., died 5 Jan 1910
at 70 yrs. 11 m. 3 d. (we did not find this
stone unless it was one of the fallen ones,
but the inscription is included in Mrs. Rowland's book).
ACKLEY, Silas W. - 1886-1919.
Hattie M. - his wife, 1886-1918.
STARBIRD, Lonnie C. - 18 Sep 1874-24 Jan 1951.
Sarah H. Cobb - his wife, 28 Jan 1874-26 Mar
1938.
Their children
Ethelyn P. - 4 Jan 1903-2 Sep 1904.
Bernard C. - 23 Apr 1901-24 Mar 1919.
Everett R. - 1864-1921.
WILLIAMS, Lincoln - 1861-1934.
Sarah R. - his wife, 1863-1912.
Steven - their son, 1880-1881.
Stephen - 1821-1893.
Eliza - his wife, 1828-1909.
Orrington - their son, 1858-1915.

Stephen — died 12 Oct 1893 at 72 yrs.
ADAMS, Clark — died 30 Apr 1881 at 77 yrs.
  Thankful — wife of Clark Adams, died 10 Mar 1871 at 70 yrs.
ELLIOTT, Mary E. Adams — "Sister," wife of Joseph R. Elliott, died 16 Sep 1886 at 48 yrs. 6 m.
OLIVER, Samuel S. — 1834-1899.
  Ellen M. — his wife, 1853-1924.
  Horace W. — their son, 1875-1891.
CURTIS, Hiram — 29 Jan 1837-8 Aug 1903.
LOTHROP, Mary Curtis — 12 Jan 1851-12 Oct 1932.
CURTIS, Infant dau — 7 Apr 1876-7 Apr 1876.
RIDLEY, James Percey — son of Humphrey & Elizabeth Ridley, died at 43 yrs. (no date of death).
  Nellie — dau of Humphrey P. & Lizzie H. Ridley died 12 May 1873 at 14 yrs. 6 m.
HARLOW, Elizabeth Ridley — wife of William Harlow, died 22 Mar 1909 at 77 yrs.
RIDLEY, Humphrey P. — died 4 Oct 1883 at 57 yrs. (there is a "Mizeph" flag).
ADAMS, Daniel — 1347-1914.
  Arvilla Williams — his wife, 1843-1909.
  Their children
  Joseph — 1880-1903.
  George — 1886-1945.
  Lydia — 1877-1962.
PATTERSON, Joseph R. — 1820-1888.
  Hannah — his wife, 1821-1913.
DAVIS, Mark C. — 27 Apr 1829-19 Dec 1887.
  Melvina A. — his wife, 1 Jan 1837-11 Aug 1897.
WILLIAMS, George W. — 19 Nov 1841-21 Sep 1892.
POWERS, Hiram D. — husband, 1843-1913.
  Sarah M. — his wife, 1840-1925.
ANDREWS, William — father, died 4 May 1868 at 78 yrs. A soldier of 1812.

Sarah - his wife, died 9 Jun 1888 at 93 yrs. 9 m.

She is waiting in the glorious Eden land which lies beyond the sunset of life.

COLEMAN, Joseph A. - son of C. R. E. & Mary Coleman, 1894-1912.

WILLIAMS, Henry H. - 1839-1896 (Civil War marker).

Adams Cemetery - from the intersection of Routes 201 and 125 in Bowdoin, go on Route 201 towards Richmond. The cemetery is on the left side of the road approximately 3 miles from the intersection of the road, just past the Adams Homestead.

EATON, Nathan - died 18 Mar 1890 at 79 yrs. 4 m. 17 d.

  How blest is our father bereft,
  Of all that could burden his mind,
  How free the soul that has left,
  This wearisome body behind.

  Sarah P. - wife of Nathan Eaton, died 23 Mar 1864 at 39 yrs.
  Elvira C. - dau of N. and Sarah P. Eaton, died 6 Feb 1864 at 16 yrs. 11 m.

  She lived as peaceful as a dove
  She died as blossoms die:
  And now her spirit floats above
  A seraph in the sky.

  Mary F. - 1852-1882.
  James E. - son of Nathan & S. Eaton, died 29 Apr 1860 at 1 yr. 3 m.
WILLIAMS, Harriet E. - dau of Otis & Caroline Williams, died 12 May 1849 at 1 yr.
  Otis - 1820-1890. Sgt Co D 3rd ME Regt - Served from Apr 24, 1861 to Jan 8, 1863.
  Caroline Adams - his wife, 1818-1881.
ADAMS, Samuel - died 10 Nov 1882 at 80 yrs. 9 m. 20 d.
  Hannah P. - his wife, died 21 Nov 1880 at 73 yrs. 7 m. 10 d.
  Harry Walton - 1858-1948.

KENDALL, Ella Adams - 1849-1932.
HINE, Erastus Walton - Killed in the Battle of the Wilderness on his 27th birthday 5 May 1864.
   Harriet Adams - his wife, born in Bowdoin, ME, 16 Nov 1838, died 25 May 1914, buried in Eureka, CA.
ADAMS, Israel G. - son of Samuel & Hannah P. Adams, died 31 Dec 1848 at 6 yrs. 3 m.
   Samuel F. - died 21 Sep 1851 at 1 yr. 13 d.
   Israel G., Capt. - died 16 Oct 1839 at 27 yrs. 11 m.
   Harriet R., Mrs. - his wife, died 5 Apr 1834 at 26 yrs. 2 d.
   Mary Elizabeth - dau of Israel G. & Hannah R. Adams died 16 Aug 1840 at 6 m.
   John R. - son of Samuel & Elizabeth Adams, 1815-1839.
   Samuel, Mr. - died 20 Aug 1840 at 83 yrs.
   Elizabeth, Mrs. - his wife, died 29 Aug 1839 at 63 yrs.
GREGORY, Gertrude D. - 1879-1964.
ADAMS, Carrie Carr - 1863-1940.
DODGE, Charles F. - 1856-1927.
   Abbie L. Adams - his wife, 1854-1942.
ADAMS, James - died 13 Dec 1855 at 63 yrs.
   Betsey - wife of James Adams formerly wife of Benj. R. Potter, died 10 Jul 1867 at 77 yrs. 3 m.
UNDERHILL, Susan - wife of Albert C. Underhill, died 20 Aug 1850 at 30 yrs.

   Though sister has gone and left here,
   She dwells an angel now on high.
   No pain or sickness can she fear,
   And death and danger may defy.

SNOW, Isaac W. - died 3 Nov 1855 at 3 m. 17 d.

Isaac W. - died 18 Sep 1859 at 2 m. 20 d.
Children of Wm. E. & Rebecca P. Snow.
Wm. E. - 1825-1903.
Rebecca P. - wife of Wm. E. Snow, 1831-1878.

If aught of goodness or of grace
Be mine, hers be the glory
She led me on in wisdom's path
And set the light before me.

CURTIS, Eben - 1829-1892.
  Mary E. - his wife, 1824-1888.
PURINTON, Granville - 1836-1885.
  Achsah - his wife, 1854-1937 (DAR marker).
  Angie - their dau, 1883-1941.
HAWKES, George A. - 1862-1935.
  Annie L. - 1859-1938 (Daughters of Union Veterans of the Civil War 1861-1865 marker).
HATCH, Lizzie E. - wife of Oscar M. Hatch, 1859-1912.
PURINTON, Clarence O. - 1864-1944.
  Lizzie A. - 1870-1902.
  Mary E. - 1841-1913.
  Abiezer P. - 1837-1917.
CARTER, John P. - 1907-1970.
  Harriet W. - wife of John Carter, 1904- .
WOODS, Victoria M. - wife of O. A. Woods, 1914- .
  Elizabeth - wife of O. A. Woods, 1911-1930.
  Orie A. - 1908- .
COOMBS, Isaac - died 16 Sep 1856 at 61 yrs. 3 m.
  Hannah A. - his wife, died 20 Dec 1889 at 80 yrs. 4 m.
  Cornelia W. - their child, died 10 Nov 1847 at 8 m.
  Israel A. - Sergt Co C 1st ME Cav, 1836-1891.
  Samuel P. - 1844-1918.
BOWIE, Harriet A. - 1834-1896.

WILSON, Johnson - my father, died 30 Mar 1857 at 81 yrs. 9 m.
NELSON, Sarah Elizabeth - wife of Samuel Nelson, 23 Sep 1858-25 Dec 1896 - Erected by her son Robert Evans.
RIDLEY, Anna Haynes - wife of Isaac H. Ridley, died 23 Aug 1913 at 75 yrs. 2 m.
Isaac H. - died 12 Oct 1903 at 62 yrs. 7 m.
NILES, Annie E. - wife of Clarence E. Niles, died 23 Jun 1892 at 28 yrs. 11 m. 18 d.
Robert - 1829-1896.
Sophia - wife of Robert Niles, 1834-1917.
BUKER, A. P. - born 3 Jan 1827, died 23 May 1887.
Lucy A. - his wife - born 20 Jan 1832, died 2 May 1900.
John F. - 10 Oct 1861-11 Feb 1932.
Bertha A. - wife of J. F. Buker, 23 Oct 1867-16 Sep 1909.
NORRIS, Ernest L. - 8 Mar 1865-7 Jul 1926.
Ida Ridley - his wife, 15 Mar 1865-18 May 1896.
CARR, Richard T. - father, died 21 Aug 1900 at 70 yrs. 10 d.
GAUBERT, Joseph A. - 1822-1904.
Lucinda - his wife, 1828-1914.
Louisa J. - 1857-1873.
BEAL, Edward A. - 24 Jan 1858-12 Jul 1936.
Laura Buker - 13 Jan 1867-
Esther M. - 2 Aug 1887-1 Oct 1887.
Edward B. - 23 Feb 1894-16 Apr 1894.
REEVES, Ethel Beal - 2 Oct 1900-
HOPKINS, Edward R. - son of Saml. & Abigail Hopkins, died 21 Jun 1834 at 10 yrs.
Samuel - died 18 Jan 1859 at 59 yrs. 7 m. 6 d.
DOYLE, Sarah J. - wife of Geo. E. Doyle, died 27 Aug 1864 at 22 yrs. 3 m. 11 d.
GARDNER, Mary H. - dau of William & Harriet Gardner, died 2 Dec 1849 at 14 yrs. 5 m. 10 d.

Mary Ann - died 13 Jul 1853 at 3 yrs. 5 m. 9 d.
Ellen Floretta - died 25 Jul 1853 at 1 y. 6 d.
Children of William R. & Harriet Gardner

GARDINER, Harriet - wife of William Gardiner, died 27 Jun 1854 at 41 yrs. 8 m.
Charles C. - died 31 Aug 1861 at 19 yrs. - a private in Company C, 3 regiment Maine (?). he gave his life a sacrifice to his Country.

THOMPSON, Julia E. - dau of Salmon H. & Emma A. Thompson, died 1 Apr 1860 at 1 yr. 2 m.
Marilla M. - died 20 Aug 1847 at 1 yr. 9 m. 15 d.
Charles L. - died 30 Dec 1841 at 1 yr. 9 m.
Children of Salmon H. & Jane Thompson.
Jane - wife of Salmon H. Thompson, died 19 Mar 1847 at 26 yrs.

CORNISH, George B. - only child of A. & B. A. Cornish, died 6 Apr 1857 at 3 m. 14 d.
James L. - only child of Abram A. & Rebecca Cornish, died 10 Apr 1856 at 1 yr. 2 m.
Lucy A. R. - dau of Abram & Rebecca Cornish, died 16 Sep 1853 at 1 yr. 7 m.

ROGERS, Lucy - wife of Col J. M. Rogers, died 18 Feb 1858 at 71 yrs. 8 m.
James M., Col. - died 26 Jun 1851 at 66 yrs. 4 m.

RIDLEY, Ambrose - died 28 Jul 1831 at 29 yrs.
Abigail - his wife, died 23 Dec 1847 at 50 yrs.
Lizzie M. - dau of Isaac H. & Anna Ridley, died 23 Feb 1839 at 19 yrs. 2 m.
Isaac - died in Bowdoin, ME, 10 Mar 1874 at 74 yrs. 8 m.
Charles S. - son of Isaac & Hannah Ridley, died 18 Nov 1841 at 11 yrs.

SNOW, John - died 29 Dec 1852 at 33 yrs.
  Ambrose H. - son of John & Elizabeth Snow,
  died 30 Dec 1848 at 19 yrs. 4 m.
  Elizabeth - wife of John Snow, died 29 May
  1869 at 81 yrs.
  John - died 8 Mar 1861 at 79 yrs. 4 m.

  Blessed are they that sleep in the Lord.

ADAMS, Sarah - wife of Isaac R. Adams, died
  21 May 1850 at 30 yrs.
  Isaac R. - died 18 Oct 1880 at 59 yrs.
  Adam - died 22 Mar 1871 at 81 yrs. 9 m.
  Ruth - wife of Adam Adams, died 13 Mar 1856
  at 64 yrs.

  Our Mother sleeps death's dreamless sleep
  Her calm and placid brow
  Clouds not amid the tears we weep
  She heeds no anguish now.

HIGGINS, Anna R. - wife of John Higgins, died
  (date and age buried in ground).
  Edward L. - son of John & Anna B. Higgins,
  died 13 Feb 1850 at 9 yrs. 1 m. 17 d.
THOMPSON, Lucy Mary - dau of Solomon E. & Susan
  Thompson, died 21 Nov 1850 at 3 yrs. 2 m.
  Susan - wife of Solomon E. Thompson, died 11
  Aug 1852 at 32 yrs. 4 m.
LEWIS, George - died 20 Jan 1848 at 82 yrs.
  Martha - wife of George Lewis, died 15 Nov
  1857 at 92 yrs.
VARNUM, Eunice - wife of Ralph Varnum, died
  19 Nov 1864 at 81 yrs. 1 m.
  Ralph - died 2 Nov 1815.
ADAMS, Harold P. - Maine Sgt 56 Pioneer Inf
  World War, 4 May 1891-21 Jun 1970.
  Margaret Holyoke - his wife, 1892-1967.

ROGERS, Lincoln E. - 19 Feb 1861-23 Jan 1950.
  Eva A. Niles - his wife, 26 Jan 1861-17
  Apr 1930.
KEMPTON, Lillian Niles - 1865-1925.
ADAMS, Walton S. - 1882-1972.
  Chastine Longley - his wife, 1888-1947.
  Ella C. Purinton - his wife, 1856-1940.
  Helen W. - 1887-1912.
  Frank Samuel, Hon. - 1852-1920.

  Representative Maine Legislature 1895
  Grandson of Samuel Adams who served
  at Valley Forge under General Washington.
  Direct descendant of Philip Adams a Freeman at York 1652.
  Erected to his memory by his brother Harry
  Walton Adams 1930.

  Herbert K. - 1892-1973.
  Lydia M. - his wife, 1892-1980.
  Helen -

Brown Cemetery - from the intersection of Routes 201 and 125, go towards Bowdoin Center and take the first right onto the Lewis Road. Go 4.9 miles on the Lewis Road. The cemetery is on the left side of the road and approximately 200 feet off the road directly beside a gravel pit. As of 1987, all stones had been destroyed except those for Captain Jonathan Brown and his wife Deborah. <u>Bowdoin Vital Records</u> show two more burials than we found stones for when we copied the inscriptions during the 1970's.

BROWN, Jonathan - in memory of Jonathan Brown, Esq (husband of Jane), who died 18 Jul 1842 at 59 yrs. 9 m.

In a good hope through grace
The King, the Begger and the Slave,
All meet at the same place.
There is no destination in the grave
Among old Adam's race.

But, when the Lord from Heaven descends
And bids all nations rise
He'll separate his chosen friends,
From all his enemies.

Margaret A. - 2nd wife of Capt. J (onathan) Brown, died 28 Aug 1883 at 70 yrs.
Jonathan - (Capt, husband Margaret A.) died 13 Sep 1886 at 73 yrs. 3 m.
Jane - wife of Jonathan, died 12 Oct 1850 at 69 yrs. 1 m (broken stone).
HAMILTON, Ella M. - wife of James H Hamilton, died 28 Aug 1886 at 22 yrs.
BROWN, Elizabeth A. - wife of John Brown (<u>Bowdoin Vital Records</u>, 1st wife of Capt

Jonathan), died 28 Sep 1877 at 70 yrs. 7 m.

Whether we live or die we are the Lords.

E. - died 18 Apr 1860 at 18 m.
Jonathan, Capt. - died 14 Jul 1837 at 84 yrs. 9 m.

(The stone is decorated with a snake holding it's tail in it's mouth.)

Deborah, Mrs. - wife of Capt Jonathan Brown, died 31 Dec 1847 at 86 yrs.
James A. - son of Jonathan and Elizabeth A. Brown, died 18 Sep 1851 at 13 m.
Maria - died 4 Dec 1856 at 35 yrs. 8 m.

Allen Family Cemetery - this burial ground is located on Route 125 between Bowdoin Center and Lisbon Falls, but only a short distance from Bowdoin Center. It is on the left side of the road and is in bad shape with fallen trees. Mrs. Leah Smith says at least one stone is missing. We entered the cemetery by going through the back yard of Mrs. Smith's home.

ALLEN, John, 2d - died 14 Jul 1870 at 53 yrs. 3 (?) m. (stone is broken).
Elijah - died 14 Mar 1851 at 84 yrs.
Jane, Mrs. - wife of Elijah Allen, died 26 Sep 1843 at 73 yrs.
John - died 4 Jun 1868 at 72 yrs. 5 m. 18 d.
Sally - wife of John Allen, died 11 Apr 1867 at 68 (?) yrs. 5 m. (stone chipped).

(Mrs. Smith thinks the missing stone was for a Mary.)

Skelton Family Cemetery - this burial ground is near the man-made Stoddard's Pond, in the corner made by Route 201 and Route 125 going towards Bowdoinham. It is well kept and fenced in by a mortared stone fence capped with cement. At one time there was a large house near the cemetery.

SKELTON, Sidney D. - 1832-1919.
Mary E. - his wife, 1839-1927.
Mary E. - dau of S. D. & M. E. Skelton, 1873-1900.

White Cemetery - from the intersection of Route 125 and the West Road (on Upper Main Street, Lisbon Falls), go 5.2 miles on the West Road. You will see a stone wall on the left going in to the woods perpendicular to the road. Follow this wall to reach the cemetery. In the 1970's when we copied these inscriptions, it was clearly obvious that there had once been many more stones than we found. There were broken stones and several stones were flat under a covering of earth. Also, the stone for Deacon Nathaniel Smith, who died in 1842, was found some distance from the cemetery and returned to the cemetery. Thusly, to give a more complete list of people buried in the White Cemetery, our list has been supplemented considerably by information from the <u>Bowdoin Vital Records</u> (referred to earlier).

WHITE, Isaac, Dea. - husband Martha, Sep 1858 at 87 yrs.
  Martha - wife of Deacon Isaac White, died 29 Jun 1856 at 86 yrs.
  Joseph - died 14 Jun 1886 at 81 yrs. 4 m.
  John - child of James & Eunice White, died 26 Aug 1839 at 26 yrs.
  Martha O. - wife of Joseph White, died 8 Jan 1884 at 77 yrs. 5 m. 8 d.
  William E. - died in Bath, 13 Feb 1873 at 38 yrs. 8 m. (His parents were Joseph & Martha O. White.)
  Joseph M. - son of Joseph and Martha O. White, died 27 Nov 1860 at 20 yrs. 6 m.
  Sanford H. - son of Joseph and Martha O. White, died 8 Nov 1852 at 15 yrs. 11 m.
  Gideon, Mr. - died 9 Nov 1836 at 42 yrs.
  Rhoda S. - wife of Gideon White, died 24 May 1849 at 49 yrs. 3 m.

James - husband of Eunice, died 15 Jan 1856 at 88 yrs.
Eunice - wife of James White, died 28 Nov 1837 at 57 yrs. (<u>Bowdoin Vital Records</u>, 1827 at 54 yrs).

The sting of death is past. The victory is obtained. At the last trumpets dreadful blast, I shall with Jesus reign.

George - son of James and Eunice White, died 20 May 1842 at 36 yrs.

Come and see the end of man,
For you must surely go,
Your life is nothing but a span,
Like all things here below.

Mary - wife of Isaac White, died 5 Dec 1858 at 57 yrs.
Isaac - husband of Mary, died 6 Apr 1864 at 61 yrs.
Chas. - father (there were no dates on the massive granite oblisk, but <u>Bowdoin Vital Records</u>, died 6 Oct 1873 at 55 yrs).
Martha W. Buker - wife of Charles White, died 9 Feb 1909 at 88 yrs.
BUKER, Lovina P. - child of James & Jane (White) Buker, died 22 Aug 1846 at 22 yrs. 10 m.
James - husband Jane, died 3 Aug 1837 at 40 yrs. 5 m.
Jane - wife of James, died 6 Oct 1886 at 90 yrs.
Sarah E. - child of Isaac W. & Mary E. (Knight) Buker, died 12 Jan 1866 at 1 yr. 7 m.
ABBOTT, Susan A. - dau of James and Sarah A. Abbott, died 21 Aug 1853 at 7 m. 15 d.
KNIGHT, Martha - wife of Daniel Knight, died

1 Oct 1841 at 56 yrs. 6 m.
Daniel - husband of Martha, died 11 Sep 1858 at 81 yrs. (Bowdoin Vital Records, 14 Sep).
WILSON, Elizabeth - wife of William Wilson, died 24 Nov 1870 at 73 yrs. 6 m.
William W. - husband of Elizabeth, died 6 Dec 1858 at 61 yrs. 8 m (Bowdoin Vital Records, 1859).
America C. - son of Wm. and Eliz. Wilson, died 27 Apr 1858 at 27 yrs. (Bowdoin Vital Records, America G.).
Asa C. - son of William and Elizabeth Wilson, died   Apr   (Bowdoin Vital Records, 9 Aug 1857 at 33 yrs.).
WHITTEN, George - died 20 Sep 1881 at 64 yrs. 2 m. 16 d.
Joseph - died 23 Oct 1852 at 78 yrs.
Thirsa R. - his wife, 1827-1900.
Walker W. - 1811-1880.
SMITH, Nath'l, Dea. - died 20 Dec 1842 at 80 yrs.
JACK, Loveria B. - dau of Hughey and Hannah Jack died 3 Mar 1850 at 2 yrs. (Bowdoin Vital Records Lovina and 8 Mar).
Roxanna S. - dau of Hugh and Hannah Jack, died 8 Dec 1862 at 20 yrs.
Hughey - died 23 Oct 1848 at 42 yrs.
TARBOX, Aaron - died 28 Jan 1880 at 79 yrs. 4 m.
Harriet - wife of Aaron Tarbox, born 1 May 1803, died 6 Jan 1896 (Bowdoin Vital Records, 1890).
FLAGG, John - husband Sarah, died 24 Dec 1859 at 73 yrs. 7 m.
William F. - child of William and Matilda Flagg, died 11 May 1892 at 45 yrs. 8 m.
Sarah - wife of John, died 24 Mar 1864 at 74 yrs. 5 m.
William - husband Matilda (no dates).

Zaelta F. - child of Jonas and Sarah A. Flagg, died 20 Sep 1849 at 9 yrs. 5 m.
Matilda - wife of William Flagg, died 1 Oct 1888 at 77 yrs. 3 m. 7 d.
Jonas - died 6 Sep 1849 at 34 yrs. 5 m.
Bradford - son of William and Matilda Flagg, died 7 Mar 1842 at 4 yrs. 6 m.

DREWITZ, Frederick Wm. - son of Frederick and S. L. Drewitz, died 19 Sep 1841 at 9 yrs. (<u>Bowdoin</u> <u>Vital</u> <u>Records</u> give initials of mother as A. L.).
Frederick Wm. - was lost at Sea Oct 1841 at 42 yrs.

ALLEN, Anna, Mrs. - wife of Eliphalet Allen, died 16 Apr 1864 at 74 yrs. 4 m.
Eliphalet - husband Anna, died 30 Jun 1852 at 66 yrs. 3 m.

MAXWELL, Theodore S. - child of Solomon and Catherine Maxwell, died 21 Jul 1850 at 38 yrs. 10 m.
Solomon - died 26 Dec 1868 at 87 yrs. 6 m. 22 d.
Catherine - his wife, died 5 Jan 1867 at 79 yrs. 2 m. 26 d.
Jane - child Solomon and Catherine Maxwell, died 5 Apr 1850 at 35 yrs. 4 m.

PRESTON, Sarah, Mrs. - wife of John O. Preston, died 2 Jun 1845 at 24 yrs. (<u>Bowdoin</u> <u>Vital</u> <u>Records</u>, Sarah (Flagg), child of John and Sarah Flagg).

RIDLEY, Philena J. - wife of John S. Ridley, died 14 Jan 1857 at 32 yrs. 6 m. 14 d (<u>Bowdoin</u> <u>Vital</u> <u>Records</u>, 1867).

Come waste your years upon this grave
My husband and children dear
For one who was beloved by all
Lies moldering here.

THURLOW, Hurbert - son of Chas. and Melisa (?) Thurlow, died 2 Sep 1861 at 5 m. (<u>Bowdoin Vital Records</u>, Herbbert and mother, Adeline (Jack)).
Hannah - wife of John Thurlow, died 19 Apr 1888 at 84 yrs. 6 m. (<u>Bowdoin Vital Records</u>, Hannah (Brimijohn), 2nd wife).
John, Jr. - husband Hannah, died 23 Sep 1869 at 78 yrs.
Sarah - 1st wife John, Jr, died 22 Jul 1851 at 54 yrs. 10 m.
HOLBROOK, Roseletta A. - dau of John K. and Sarah Holbrook, died 7 Aug 1858 at 4 yrs. 11 m. 7 d.
Sarah - wife of John K. Holbrook, died 28 Oct 1864 at 39 yrs. 3 m. 8 d.
COOMBS, Mary F. - wife of Charles R. Coombs, died 8 Jun 1889 at 54 yrs.
CHASE, Sumner - son of James, 2d and Louisa, died 20 Jan 1846 at 5 m.

Leonard Family Cemetery - at Bowdoin Center, take the Meadow Road and go .5 of a mile. Turn left on a dirt road which leads to the cemetery.

LEONARD, Seth H. - 1821-1886.
  Philena B. - his wife, 1829-1866.
  Ruth C. Britt - his wife, 1833-1919.
  Melvin S. - 1845-1862.
  Isaac - 1779- .
  Margaret - his wife, 1783- .
  Their sons
  Robert H. - 1819- .
  Alexander P. - 1825- .
ANDERSON, Parker - son of Chas. M. Anderson & Lena B. Leonard, 20 Jun 1894-25 Sep 1913.
  Lena B. Leonard - wife of Chas. M. Anderson, 24 Jan 1870-21 Jan 1928.
  Charles M. - 19 Aug 1865-7 Mar 1905.
  Vincent F. - 14 Oct 1861-21 Nov 1919.
  Sarah E. Mountfort - wife of Cornelius T. Anderson, 1 Oct 1830-11 Nov 1906.
  Cornelius T. - 27 Aug 1826-11 Jan 1920.
LUCE, William D. - 25 Mar 1861-25 Apr 1928. Co D 3rd NY Regt BPOE Cuba, Porto Rico, USA, Philippine Islands, United Spanish War Veteran, 1898-1902.
  Annie M. Anderson - wife of Wm. D. Luce, 1859-1943.

Temple/Randall Cemetery - from the intersection of Routes 201 and 125, go 4.2 miles on Route 201 towards Richmond. The cemetery is on the right in the woods and on a hill. It adjoins the Bowdoinham Town line.

TEMPLE, Geo. F. - 1825-1906.
  Zilpha A. - wife of Geo. F. Temple, 1825-1893.

Lucy - wife of Abijah Temple, died 16 Jan 1868 at 74 yrs. 8 m.
Abijah - died 4 Jan 1859 at 66 yrs.
John, Lieut. - died 13 Jan 1842 at 85 yrs.
Mary - wife of John Temple, died 23 Nov 1846 at 90 yrs.
John, Jr. - died 7 Jul 1802 at 15 yrs. 5 m.
Cyrus, II - son of Abijah & Lucy Temple, died 6 Aug 1849 at 27 yrs. (Mrs. Rowland says Cyrus H).
Mar (ia) (J) - dau of A & L Temple (stone broken and no further data readable, but Mrs. Rowland says Maria J died at 26 yrs.).
John F. - father, 1820-1895.
Elizabeth - mother, wife of John F. Temple, 1821-1888.

Waiting in the light beyond.

John C. F. - (nothing further readable, but Mrs. Rowland says son of J & Elizabeth died 13 Mar 1885 at 23 yrs).
Cherrie - (nothing further readable, but Rowland says dau J F & Elizabeth, died 2 Aug 1880 at 20 yrs.).
Lizzie R. - died 5 Oct 1860 at 2 yrs. 7 m.
Lucy E. - died 27 Sep 1860 at 4 yrs. 7 m.
Children of John & Elizabeth Temple.

Sleep loved ones, thy suffering all are o'er
Cain ne'er again can leave thy breast
Nor anguish wake thy spirit more
From its eternal quiet rest.

Carrie D. - died 13 Oct 1860 at 8 yrs. 6 m.
John E. - died 5 Oct 1860 at 6 yrs. 7 m.
Children of John F. & Elizabeth R. Temple.

Bright beautiful beings, we miss you on
  earth.
We list for the sound of your innocent
  mirth;
The angels have borne you in silence away,
For us there are shadows, for you there
  is day.

Fannie M. - dau of John & Elizabeth Temple,
  17 Feb 1849-3 Feb 1903.
Albert F. - 17 Mar 1862-17 Oct 1904.
LANCASTER, Sarah, Mrs. - consort of Mr. Daniel
  Lancaster, died 13 Nov 1803 at 37 yrs.

Farewell my kind and loving mate.
Jesus calls I cannot wait.
Down in the grave my body lies,
I rest with God up in the skies.

PARLIN, Sarah, Mrs. - wife of Mr. Josiah Parlin,
  died 12 Sep 1808 at 74 yrs.
Mary - died 13 Nov 1846 at 85 yrs.
RANDALL, Albion Q., A. M. - a Graduate of
  Bowdoin College Class of 1852, died 28 Mar
  1878 at 49 yrs.
Hatherly - son of Hatherly & Elizabeth Randall
  died 1 Nov 1802 at 5 m. 25 d.
Hatherly, Capt. - died 19 Apr 1858 at 92 yrs.
  7 m. 23 d.
Elizabeth, Miss - dau of Capt Hatherly
  Randall, died 3 Oct 1820 at 21 yrs.
Elisabeth, Mrs. - consort of Capt Hatherly
  Randall, died 28 Oct 1809 at 47 yrs.
Susanna, Mrs. - consort of Capt. Hatherly
  Randall, died 15 Apr 1814 at 41 yrs.
  (Two infants lie by her side.)
Benjamin, Jr. - died 26 Mar 1876 at 50 yrs.

Dear Brother, thou hast gone to rest.
Thy troubles now are o'er.
Oh help us to be reconciled.
Since we meet thee here, no more.

George N. - son of Samuel W & Courtney Randall, died 5 Jan 1862 at 3 yrs. 6 m. 14 d.
Amanda Purington - inf dau of S W & C Randall, died 21 Dec 1864.
Courtney - wife of Samuel W Randall and dau of Capt Humphrey & Rebecca Purington, died 11 May 1870 at 38 yrs. 6 m. 28 d.
Samuel W. - died 18 Nov 1898 at 70 yrs.
Amanda - wife of Samuel W Randall, died 19 Apr 1903 at 69 yrs. 7 m.
Benjamin, Maj. - father, 17 Feb 1793-24 Jun 1870.
Charity - mother, 29 Dec 1797-16 Apr 1826, wife of Benjamin.
Lucy - wife of Benj Randall died 4 May 1886 at 85 yrs. 7 m. 5 d.
MARINER, Sarah Randall - mother, wife of John H Mariner, died 21 May 1914 at 75 yrs. 9 d.
John H. - father, died 13 Jan 1890 at 37 yrs. 15 d.

Wheeler Family Cemetery - go 3.5 miles on the West Road from the intersection of Route 125 (Upper Main St, Lisbon Falls) and the West Road. Turn right into the driveway of the Wheeler Homestead and go up a hill; the burial lot is on a rise of land between the Wheeler Homestead and a second Wheeler home. When we copied the inscriptions in 1972, Doris (Wheeler) Gagne said the homestead was built by Joseph Wheeler and has been occupied by members of the family continuously except for about a year following the death of Alfred T. Wheeler in 1920.

WHEELER, Tamson – wife of Joseph Wheeler, died 22 May 1871 at 71 yrs. 5 m. 17 d.
Joseph – died 30 Sep 1881 at 81 yrs. 3 m.

We'll join you in that heavenly land
No more to take the parting hand.

Simon – son of Tamson and Joseph, died 22 Jul 1871 at 50 yrs. 10 m. 23 d.
Actor – died 8 Jan 1885 at 50 yrs. 7 m. 14 d.
(There is a GAR marker.)

His toils are past his work is done,
He fought the fight, the victory won.

Infant son – of A & E J Wheeler died 1 Sep (no year; inscription on Actor's stone).
Elizabeth J. – died 28 Jul 1904 at 65 yrs.
(Mrs. Gagne says Elizabeth was the wife of Actor Wheeler, her maiden name was Polley, and she was born in Wales, England.)
Delia A. – dau of A & E Wheeler, died 6 Mar 1882 at 19 yrs. 11 m.
Hiram A. – son of A & E Wheeler, died 1 Apr 1892 at 28 yrs.
(The following were children of Actor and Elizabeth Wheeler.)
Hannah E. – died 10 Nov 1900 at 33 yrs.
Oscar D. – 26 Oct 1878-25 Jun 1905.
William D. – 29 Aug 1881-5 Aug 1912.
Alfred T. – 1874-1920.
(There are two infants buried on this lot, their graves marked by field stones, but it is not known by the family who they were.)

Buker Cemetery – this cemetery is on Haigh Mountain. From the intersection of Routes 201 and 125, go towards the Town of Richmond approximately 2 9/10ths of a mile and turn left on the Adams Road. Take the first left into the woods. We doubt one could drive to the cemetery but would have to walk, as this road is old and in bad condition. Go two or three miles. Turn right on the intersecting road, and the cemetery is on the left, surrounded by a stone wall with an iron gate. It is in very good condition for an old, abandoned cemetery. At one time there were a number of homes on Haig Mountain, and we were able to locate several old foundations.

STARBIRD, Lucinda M. – wife of Wm H Starbird, died 2 Sep 1881 at 27 yrs.
  Charlie A. – son of W H and L M Starbird, died 9 Aug 1881 at 1 yr. 14 d.

  Thy will be done.

BUKER, Esther F. – wife of John C. Buker, died 17 May 1895 at 55 yrs. 5 m. 14 d.

  She hath done what she could.

  John C. – died 1 Feb 1873 at 38 yrs.

  My Trust is in the Lord.

REED, Frank – died 12 Nov 1863 at 25 yrs.
  Abby – his wife, died 6 Apr 1892 at 61 yrs. 2 m. 21 d.
CAMPBELL, George – died 28 May 1820 at 62 yrs. 4 m. 3 d.
  Phidelia – his wife, died 2 Feb 1873 at 63 yrs.

HAWKES, Cora A. - dau of A and E E Hawkes, died 17 Sep 1863 at 3 wks. 3 d.
Eunice E. - wife of Albert Hawkes, died 7 Dec 1864 at 29 yrs. 27 d.
Albert - died 12 Aug 1889 at 55 yrs.
Mary M. - died 17 Nov 1866 at 7 m.
(There are at least five field stones.)

BUKER, Mary E. - dau of Frederic and Esther Buker, died 10 Jan 1871 at 28 yrs. 2 m. 5 d.

Her soul too pure for worlds like this
Has flown to realms of endless bliss
We hope again in Heaven to meet
And live in love at Jesus feet.

Esther - mother, wife of Frederick Buker, died 8 May 1884 at 83 yrs. 10 m.

Our Mother
Sainted name and holy one
She sleeps her life's work fully done
Her armor dropped.

George W. - member of Co. A 6 Regt and son of Frederick and Esther Buker, died 28 Jun 1863 at 25 yrs. 10 m. (he was discharged for disability).

Back from that Southern land
We welcomed him with fond hearts beating high
But oh! the spoiler was so hard
He only came to die.

Frederick - father, died 18 May 1879 at 78 yrs. 6 m.

Niles Cemetery - this cemetery is on Haig Mountain. From the intersection of Routes 201 and

125, go 2.8 miles towards the Town of Richmond. Turn left on the Adams Road. Take first road at left into the woods (see Buker Cemetery). Go two or three miles and turn left on the intersecting road. The cemetery is on the right side of the road near the old Tarr Mill ruins.

TARR, James W. - son of Wm. & Rebecca Tarr, died 31 Dec 1858 at 14 yrs. 6 m. 17 d.
  Edward - son of William & Rebecca Tarr, died 6 Sep 1861 at 19 yrs.
  Rebecca - wife of William Tarr, died 26 Jun 1860 at 58 yrs.
  William - 1798-1879.
  Martha A. - wife of Elisha Tarr, died 8 Sep 1864 at 23 yrs. 9 m. 26 d.
NILES, Emma F. - dau of Frederick & Abigail Niles, died 1 Oct 1864 at 19 yrs. 10 m.

  Dearest Emma thou hast left us,
  And thy loss we deeply feel;
  But 'tis God that hath bereft us,
  He can all our sorrow heal.

  William - 15th ME Reg't, died at Matagorda, Texas, 29 Dec 1863 at 28 yrs. 3 m.

  The loud drum shall call thee to battle
    no more
  The victory is won. Life's battle is
    o'er;
  The captain hath called thee to receive
    thy reward,
  An eternal home with the soldiers of God.

  Frederick - 1799-1869.
  Abigail - wife of Frederick, died 26 Jan 1851

at 48 yrs. 5 m.

Ward Cemetery – this cemetery is on Haig Mountain. The inscriptions were copied by Marilyn Garrity and given to us. Instructions for finding the cemetery are taken from those written by Mrs. Garrity. At Richmond Corners, take Route 197 towards Litchfield. Go about 2 miles to Dead River Road and turn left. Go 1/2 mile until the road forks to two roads on the left. Take the first one, a very sharp left called the Ward Road. Go about 2 1/2 miles and on the left there is a stone wall perpendicular to the road (difficult to find). Follow the wall into the woods for 1/4 mile through swampy land overgrown with alders, etc. The wall falls away in several places, but go straight. You will come to higher ground, and there you will find the cemetery.

WARD, John – (no dates).
  Sally – his wife – (no dates).
  Eliza – dau of J Ward (no dates).
  George – Aug 1900.
  Susan – his wife, Dec 1888.
  Eliza I. – (no dates).
  Edward – 1844-1846.
  George – 1848-1873.
  John A. – 1850-1851.
  Ruth E. – 1856-1869.
  Alonzo – 12 Mar 1858-29 Aug 1858.
  Susan J. – 8 Feb 1862.
  Children of G. and S. Ward.
  George – 26 Jul 1821-25 Aug 1900.

A honest man the noblest work of God.

Susan - mother, wife of George Ward, 26
Apr 1818-27 Dec 1888.
George C. - son of J B & F Ward, 1878-1879.

Town Grant Cemetery - this cemetery is on Haigh
Mountain. From the intersection of Routes 201
and 125, go towards Bowdoin Center approximately .5 of a mile. Turn right on the Lewis
Road. Go almost to the end of the road and
take the last right before the end. Go a
short distance, and you will be on Haig Mountain. Turn left. There is a stone wall around
the cemetery. It seems highly probable that
there were many more stones which no longer
exist, and in fact broken stones were found.

BUKER, Alvah J., Rev. - died 17 Feb 1892 at 74
  yrs. 11 m. 20 d.
  Hannah E. - wife of Rev Alvah J Buker, died
  4 Apr 1877 at 60 yrs. 3 m. 20 d.
CURTIS, Eben - died 14 Apr 1838 at 66 yrs.
  Elizabeth - wife of E Curtis, died 13 Nov
  1851 at 74 yrs.
  Mercia L. - dau of Eben & E Curtis, died
  9 Jan 1850 at 32 yrs.
POTTER, Rebecca A. - mother, wife of John M
  Potter, died 26 Nov 1886 at 50 yrs.
  John M. - father, died 23 Jan 1885 at 70 yrs.
  Achsah - wife of John M Potter, died 1 Oct
  1863 at 54 yrs.
BRIRY, Esther - wife of James Briry, died 2 Jan
  1846 at 61 yrs. 8 m.
FOSTER, Pelatiah H. - died 9 Mar 1884 at 56 yrs.
  6 m. (Masonic emblem).
  Elizabeth B. - wife of P H Foster, died 15
  May 1887 at 65 yrs.
  Sanford - son of Pelatiah and Elizabeth
  Foster, died 24 Aug 1852 at 10 m. 21 d.

BUKER, Willie - son of Charles & Susan Buker, died 12 Jul 1855 at 5 m.
BOEW, Otis A. - died 10 Aug 1851 at 2 yrs. 3 m.
William H. - died 11 Apr 1848 at 4 m. 11 d.
Children of Samuel and Driscilla S Boew.
TOWNS, Esther A. - dau of Samuel and Rhoda Towns, died 3 Aug 1853 at 20 yrs.
POTTER, James - died 3 May 1860 at 88 yrs. 3 m.
Susan - wife of James Potter, died 27 Aug 1872 at 86 yrs. 8 m. - erected by W Potter.

Campbell Cemetery - this cemetery is at the base of Haigh Mountain. From the intersection of Routes 201 and 125, go towards the Town of Richmond 2.8 miles and turn left on the Adams Road. Go approximately .2 of a mile and turn left. After a short walk, you will be at the cemetery, which is surrounded by a stone wall.

CAMPBELL, George W. - a deaf mute artist, died 26 Feb 1868 at 81 yrs.
_____ - father (no first name), died 18 Jul 1882 at 84 yrs.
_____ - mother (no first name), died 15 Sep 1882 at 84 yrs.
Geo. W. - died 30 Apr 1832 at 32 yrs.
WILLIAMS, John G. - son of Allen & Charlotte C Williams, died 25 Jun 1852 at 20 m.
Charlotte Campbell - wife of Allen T. Williams, died 5 Oct 1851 at 25 yrs. 16 d.
Allen F. - died 3 Jan 1861 at 35 yrs. 6 m.
(There are three unmarked field stones.)

Gowell Cemetery - from the intersection of Routes 201 and 125, go 1.7 miles towards Topsham. Turn right towards Trailer Park, and the burial ground is a short distance down the road on the right. It is highly probable that there were once more stones.

GOWELL, Marcia - dau of William & Abigail Gowell died 1 Oct 1851 at 5 yrs. 7 m. (dates from Bowdoin Vital Records).
Oscar - son of William & Abigail Gowell, died 6 Oct 1851 at 3 yrs. 2 m.
Anna - wife of William Gowell, died 11 Apr 1858 at 78 yrs. 4 m.
William - died 30 Sep 1851 at 78 yrs.

Gowell Burial Ground - go towards Topsham 1.6 miles from the intersection of Routes 201 and 125. This burial ground is just beyond the intersection of Route 201 with Route 138, at the left, up a hill behind the second house.

GOWELL, John - died 26 Jun 1856 at 80 yrs. 3 m.

Oh weep not for me unkindness to weep,
The weary weak body hath fallen asleep;
No more of fatigue or endurance it knows,
Oh weep not, or break not the perfect repose.

Asenath - wife of John Gowell, died 25 Apr 1849 at 73 yrs.
Wiman Woodbry - son of Wiman & Lovina Gowell, died 24 Sep 1849 at 1 yr. 9 m. 28 d.
Sawtell - son of Wiman & Lovina Gowell, died 2 Oct 1849 at 4 yrs. 28 d.
Johnson - son of Wiman & Lovina Gowell, died 11 Dec 1841 at 2 yrs. 19 d.

Buker Allen Cemetery - go 4.1 miles on the Lewis Road towards Litchfield. Take a right dirt drive into the yard of a house. Park there and then walk a very short distance. Cemetery is on a hill at the right.

BUKER, Amy P. - dau of Zaccheus & Elizabeth Buker, died 25 Jul 1832 at 26 yrs.
  Betsey, Mrs. - wife of Zaccheus Buker, died 13 Jun 1857 at 66 yrs.
  Everett W. - son of Rev Alvah J & Mrs Hannah E. **Buker**, died 26 Feb 1847 at 3 yrs.
ALLEN, Susan - dau of James M. & Adeline Allen, died 14 Oct 1848 at 3 yrs. 11 m.

Bickford Burial Ground - go .6 miles from Bowdoin Center towards Lisbon Falls on Route 125. This grave is in the back and at the right of a house. It has been ascertained that Levi had a wife and children, but his wife is buried other than with him.

BICKFORD, Levi - born 1836, died 11 Oct 1903, Pvt Civil War.

Jones Cemetery - at Bowdoin Center turn from Route 125 onto the Litchfield Road. Go 5.7 miles and turn left into a driveway. The cemetery is in about 300 feet and on the right.

JONES, Isaac - died 25 Aug 1838 at 80 yrs.
  Jane - his wife died 6 Feb 1832 at 57 yrs.
  Polly - died 19 Jun 1798 at 2 yrs. 9 m.
  Isaac - died 3 Jul 1797.
  Polly - died 18 Sep 1799.
  Children of Isaac & Jane Jones.
  Wm. K. - died 8 Nov 1881 at 72 yrs. 3 m. 2 d.
  Wm. F. - died 7 Apr 1882 at 63 yrs. 2 m. 6 d.

Grover Cemetery - at Bowdoin Center turn from Route 125 onto the Litchfield Road. Go 2.6 miles towards Litchfield. The cemetery is on the right behind a large cape style house.

GROVER, Hannah - wife of Capt B Grover, died 14 Apr 1868 at 64 yrs. 6 m.
Benj., Capt. - died 11 Dec 1879 at 78 yrs. 11 m.
Hannah - dau of Capt B & Hannah Grover, died 10 Jun 1867 at 41 yrs.
Herbert D. - son of Geo T & Abbie Grover, died 23 Jul 1882 at 3 m. 28 d.
Abbie V. - wife of George T Grover, died 10 Jun 1882 at 20 yrs. 7 d.

Lewis Cemetery - from the intersection of Routes 201 and 125, take 125 towards Bowdoin Center .5 of a mile. The cemetery is on the right almost across from a house.

LEWIS, Benjamin B. - son of Thomas & Martha Lewis, died 20 Sep 1849 at 3 yrs. 2 m.
Thomas M. - died 4 Mar 1856 at 62 yrs. 7 m.

Thus one by one earths loves do pass
From out our sight to that eternal day
What pains and tears with all their wrecking
  strife
Shall scathe them not in that serener life
Where eyes long dimmed within this nether
  sphere
Shall gaze with clearest vision where no
  tear
Will mist the scenes presented to ther view
Far peace will strew their path like
  Herman's dew
There they shall toil with sweet angelic
  cheer

There no perplexing tempter makes them fear
God's blest angels each loved one will
Passing through the death gate to eternity.

Martha R. - wife of Thomas S Lewis, died 22 May 1851 at 30 yrs. 2 m.
Thomas S. - 1820-1900.
Marcella M. - wife of Joseph E Lewis, died 22 Jun 1892 at 48 yrs. 5 m.
Margaret M. - wife of Joseph E Lewis, 1866- .
Ruth F. - wife of Thomas M Lewis, died 19 Jan 1863 at 62 yrs. 2 m. 17d.

Foster Burial Lot - from the intersection of Routes 201 and 125, go on Route 125 towards Bowdoin Center. Turn right on the Lewis Road and go .5 of a mile. The burial lot is behind the Harlan Hatch home. There is now only one stone with an inscription and several field stones. At one time there were many stones on this site, which was adjacent to the orgiinal First Baptist Church which burned in the 1830's.

FOSTER, Benjamin - son of Benjamin & Anna Foster, died 2 Jan 1822 at 9 yrs.

Small Cemetery - from Bowdoin Center go 1.6 miles towards Litchfield on the Litchfield Road. This cemetery is next to the site of the Bowdoin Town House which burned several years ago and overlooking Ceasar's Pond.

SMALL, Ebenezer, Mr. - died 18 Nov 1831 at 55 yrs.
Jane - wife of Ebenr, died 28 Nov 1838 at 54 yrs.

A Mr. Folsom copied the inscriptions in this cemetery in 1915 and found the following on a broken stone:

SMALL, Elizabeth - died 5 May 1835 at 19 yrs.

Grover Cemetery - Take the Litchfield Road at Bowdoin Center and go 3.2 miles. Take first left after Caesar's Pond. The cemetery is across from the first house on this road, a brick house on the right side of the road.

GROVER, Ester M. - wife of King T Grover, died 5 Oct 1876 at 43 yrs. 10 m. 6 d.

   We mourn thy loss dear sister
   We miss thy smiling face
   And feel that earth without thee
   Is but a desert place.

King T. - died 10 Mar 1875 at 40 yrs. 2 m.

   A husbon that was true to a wife so kind
   A son that was kind to a mother that loved him
   A brother that was loved lies sleeping here
   Till jesus shall come and awake him.

Orington H. - died 1 Dec 1858 at 30 yrs. 4½ m.
James J. - died 11 Dec 1852 at 22 yrs. 5 m.

   Adieu, adieu dear son
   I give thee up to God.

Hannah - died 21 Jul 1886 at 87 yrs. 4 m, mother.
James - died 26 Mar 1859 at 57 yrs, father.
Mary E. - died 26 Mar 1844 at 25 yrs. 9 m.

Andre J. - died at sea 8 Feb 1845 at 18 yrs. 5 m.
Martha - wife of George N Grover, died 18 Jul 1855 at 17 yrs. 8 d.
Winfield N. - son of George N & Martha Grover, died 10 Mar 1879 at 24 yrs.
Fairfield - son of James & Hannah Grover, died 23 Apr (?) 1842 at 2 yrs. 9 m.
Sarah H. - died 7 Sep 1850 at 9 yrs 1 m.
King T. - died 11 Dec 1858 at 4 m.
Frederick - died 28 May 1861 at 1 yr. 6 m.
P. -   (small stones with initials P. G.
J. -   and J. G. - no dates).
BUBIER, Susan - died 26 Dec 1877 at 95 yrs.

Williams Family Cemetery - from the intersection of Routes 201 and 125, go 2.8 miles towards Richmond. Turn left on the Adams Road and go to the home of Mrs. Vesta Williams (widow of Carroll). The house is on the right and the cemetery is behind it. The house was moved to its present location and was originally the East Bowdoin Chapel. When we copied the inscriptions on 14 October 1972, Mr. and Mrs. Williams went to the cemetery with us and explained the relationships.

WILLIAMS, Charles E. - 1871-1926.
Addie A. - his wife (no dates when copied, but we understand 1859-Nov 1946 has now been inscribed. Bowdoin Town Report for Year Ending 10 Feb 1938 states she was born 7 Apr 1859. Family member says family record says 7 Apr 1867). (Carroll Williams' parents)
Ruby May - 1898-1914 (Carroll's sister).
Eddie - 1876-1894 (cousin to Carroll; Eddie's parents were Minot and Lucy Williams).

Mary A. - mother, wife of Joel Williams, 30
May 1824-7 Feb 1898.
Joel - father, 25 Sep 1820-11 Feb 1896,
P of H (grandparents of Carroll on mother's
side; his mother was a Williams and married
a Williams).
Mary - wife of John Williams, died 19 Jan
1861 at 81 yrs. 9 m.
John - died 20 Aug 1855 at 78 yrs. (Mary and
John were Joel Williams' parents).

Humphrey Purinton Burial Lot - go .4 of a mile
on Route 125 towards Bowdoin Center. Turn right
onto the Lewis Road and go 3.2 miles. The
burial lot is on the left and surrounded by a
stone wall.

PURINTON, John A. - son of Humphrey & Harriet
  Purinton, died 14 Jun 1859 at 19 yrs. 4 m.
  Humphrey, Esq. - died 19 Mar 1855 at 51 yrs.

Bubier-Cripps Cemetery - at Bowdoin Center, take
the road to Litchfield and go towards Litchfield
about 4.4 miles. Turn left onto a side road and
the cemetery is on the right.

CRIPPS, George H., Mr. - died 19 Oct 1892 at
  74 yrs. 5 m.
  Hannah - wife, died 25 Apr 1867 at 39 yrs.
  10 m.
BUBIER, William, Mr. - died 15 Sep 1844 at 79
  yrs.
  Sarah - wife, died 13 Nov 1836 at 71 yrs.

Jacques Cemetery - this cemetery is .7 of a mile
from the intersection of Routes 201 and 125 going
from Bowdoin to Topsham and in the corner made by
the McIver Road and Route 201. The inscriptions

were copied during the 1970's. Many stones were broken and toppled, and it was clearly evident that there had once been more stones. A numer of people through the years have copied the inscriptions in this cemetery, and we have access to some of these and have endeavored to clarify any differences.

TARR, Mary, Mrs. - widow of Mr. Daniel B. Tarr, who perished at sea Aug 1827, and dau of Rev. Humphrey & Mrs Thankful Purinton, died 12 Nov 1835 at 39 yrs.
PURINTON, Humphrey, Rev. - died 28 Jan 1832 at 73 yrs.
  Thankful, Mrs. - relict of Rev Humphrey Purinton, died 23 Jan 1835 at 74 yrs.
RANDALL, Thankful, Mrs. - wife of Isaac Randall, died 22 Mar 1834 at 53 yrs.
  Joseph - son, died at Wilmington, NC, 31 Dec 1840 at 22 yrs.
  Lincoln - son, died at sea 25 Oct 1841, Lat 26, Long 63½, at 20 yrs.
  Isaac - died 27 May 1852 at 76 yrs.
PURINTON, Mary, Mrs. - wife of Elder Stephen Purinton, died 9 Jan 1835 at 37 yrs. Also her inf aged 9 d.
JACQUES, Hepsibeth, Miss - dau of Johnson & Hannah Jacques, died 28 Mar 1834 at 18 yrs.
  Johnson, Hon. - died 16 Nov 1851 at 65 yrs. 10 m.
SKELTON, Sybel - wife of Robert Skelton, died 6 Jan 1868. (The <u>Bowdoin</u> <u>Vital</u> <u>Records</u> say at age 43 and give birth date of 16 Nov 1819, and the 1850 Census shows her age then as 31.)
JACQUES, Elizabeth - wife of Dea Benj Jacques, died 15 Feb 1849 at 88 yrs. 10 m.
  Nathaniel, Mr. - died 20 Nov 1836.
GOWELL, Samuel - died 16 Mar 1880 at 76 yrs.
  Melinda - wife of Samuel Gowell, died 28 Apr

1879 at 71 yrs. 2 m. (<u>Bowdoin Vital Records</u> show age at death of 91 yrs. 2 m; however <u>Ancestor Richard Gowell and His Descendants</u> by Rev. Chas N Sinnett says Samuel married Melinda Purinton, dau of Nathaniel L. and Hepsabah Purinton, and this lady was born 16 Feb 1868, per Bowdoin records which did not burn).

Hepzabah - wife of Capt Nath'l Purinton, died 18 Jun 1841 at 81 yrs.

John, Mr. - died 2 Nov 1836 at 35 yrs.

SKELTON, Hannah J. - dau of Robert M & Sybel Skelton, died 15 Aug 1869 at 26 yrs. (<u>Bowdoin Vital Records</u> show age at death as 20 yrs, but 1850 Census shows Hannah as 7 then).

Richard F. - son of Robert M & Sybel Skelton, died 28 Jun 1870/78 at 19 yrs. 8 m. 5 d.

Johnson J. - died 24 Jul 1864 at 18 yrs. 4 m.

Robert H. - died 15 Nov 1863 at 11 yrs. 8 m. (Stone shows Robert and Johnson as children of Robert and Sybel Skelton.)

PURINTON, Mary O. - wife of John L. Purinton, died 24 Jul 1879 at 40 yrs.

John L. - died 28 Sep 1877 at 42 yrs. 2 m.

My kind loving wife & daughter so dear
Come cease your sad weeping and dry your
 tears
That bright golden city is clear to my view
Its portals are open I'll wait there for
 you.
Earths mission is ended. I know that sweet
 voice
Jesus is calling come home and rejoice.

THORN, Barnett - died 1 Jun 1887 at 83 yrs. 3 m. (<u>Bowdoin Vital Records</u>, 4 Jun 1887 at 88 yrs. 3 m.).

Jane - wife of Barnett Thorn, died 25
1861 at 37 yrs. (Bowdoin Vital Records,
26 Mar 1861 at 57 yrs.).

PURINTON, Hattie A. - dau of John L. & Mary O.
Purinton, died 3 May 1879 at 17 yrs. 2 m.

> Here sleeps my darling Hattie
> Whose mission early done
> In life's bright noontide perished
> Like shadows in the sun.

PURRINTON, Nath'l, Capt. - died 13 Jun 1832
at 75 yrs.

COOMBS, Mary F. - wife of Chas. B. Coombs,
died 8 Jun 1889 at 51 yrs.

Ephraim Small Cemetery - from the intersection of Routes 201 and 125, go 1.3 miles on Route 201 towards the Town of Richmond. Turn right on road just before Adams Homestead and go about 1 mile.

SMALL, Amos, Jr., Mr. - died at Dobay Island
Darien (Bowdoin Vital Records "on the
Carolina Coast") 25 Sep 1846 at 20 yrs. 6 m.

Mercy - wife of Dea Amos Small died 14 Apr
1852 at 51 yrs.

(No stone is now found for Amos, Sr., but
Bowdoin Vital Records state he died 18 Jan
1884 on "his father's homestead.")

Ruth - dau of A & M. Small, died 3 Aug 1833
at 2 yrs. 4 m.

Mary E. - dau of A & M Small, died 24 Mar
1842 at 8 yrs.

Dorcas, Mrs. - wife of Ephraim Small, died
2 Oct 1847 at 84 yrs. 6 m.

Ephraim, Mr. - died 8 Jan 1842 at 82 yrs. 2 m.

Thomas Skelton Family Cemetery - from the intersection of Routes 201 and 125, go .3 of a mile towards Topsham. The cemetery is at the left and as of 1992 near a trailer home.

MESERVE, Hettie E. - dau of A C G & Dorcas J Meserve, died 16 Feb 1882 at 21 yrs 10 m.
  Susie E. - dau of A. C. G. & Dorcas J. Meserve, died 1 Apr 1880 at 18 yrs 3 m.
  Dorcas J. - wife of A. C. G. Meserve, died 24 Mar 1879 at 48 yrs. (Dorcas was dau of Thomas Skelton).
GRAVES, Frances E. - wife of Wm. A. Graves, died 24 Oct 1865 at 27 yrs 1 m. (Frances was dau of Thomas Skelton).
SKELTON, Thomas - 1807-1882.
  Mehetable T. - wife of Thomas Skelton, 1808-1873.

Elliott Cemetery (also known as Eaton and Coombs Cemetery) - from the intersection of Routes 201 and 125, go .7 of a mile towards the Town of Richmond. Turn left and go a short distance to an old church. The cemetery is next to the church.

RANDALL, Joseph, Mr. - died 7 Aug 1818 at 63 yrs.
  Martha, Mrs. - his wife, died 25 Feb 1844 at 86 yrs.

  The sweet remembrance of the just
  Shall flourish when they sleep in dust
  (epitaph on double stone for Joseph and Martha Randall).

EATON, Solomon - died 3 Oct 1856 at 82 yrs.

Solomon - son of Solomon Eaton, Esqr, died 27 Feb 1815 at 2 yrs.
Peggy, Mrs. - wife of Solomon Eaton, died 15 Sep 1843 at 65 yrs.
Rowland L., Mr. - A member of the sophomore class Bowdoin College, died 10 Jun 1833 at 22 yrs.
LEONARD, Eliza E., Mrs. - wife of Abiel Leonard, died 11 Jul 1832 at 27 yrs.

Rest sister spirit farewell awhile
Thou friend to memory dear
Tis thine to know the seraphs smile
Thy home a brighter sphere.

Abiel, Col. - died 17 Sep 1843 at 37 yrs.
WILSON, Isaac - 2 Jul 1824-26 Jul 1899.
Eliza E. Leonard - his wife, 5 Jul 1832- 18 Jan 1899.
RANDALL, Susan R., Mrs. - wife of Capt Otis Randall, died 21 Sep 1843 at 33 yrs. 11 m. (The stone states that Capt. Otis Randall died at sea 5 Jun 1847 at 36 yrs.)
WILSON, Lucy - (this stone has nothing on it but the name "Lucy" and is behind the Isaac Wilson stone).
PATTERSON, Elisha E. - son of Col E & Charity E Patterson, died 29 Jun 1833 at 1 yr. 1 m.
Elisha, Col. - died 19 May 1860 at 66 yrs.
Charity E. - wife of Col Elisha Patterson, died 25 Apr 1868 at 71 yrs. 5 m.
RANDALL, Foster, Esq. - died 21 Jul 1842 at 32 yrs. 10 m. 21 d.
PURINGTON, Marget, Mrs. - wife of Rev Collamore Purington, formerly widow of Capt Foster Randall, died 16 Jun 1855 at 39 yrs. 5 m. 16 d.

The pleasures of earth do soon fade away
They bloom for a season and then they decay
But pleasures more lasting in Jesus are given
Salvation on earth and a mansion in heaven.

HORN, Charity, Miss - died 29 Dec 1837 at 72 yrs.
PATTERSON, George F. - son of Col Elisha & Charity E Patterson, died 3 Nov 1861 at 24 yrs. 2 m.
  Nancy M. - dau of Col Elisha & Charity E Patterson, died 24 Jan 1862 at 34 yrs. 8 m.
BOOMER, Eliza - wife of Joel S. Boomer, died 5 Jan 1865 at 23 yrs. 9 m. 18 d.
WILLIAMS, George - entered into rest 3 Sep 1870 at 27 yrs.

He is not lost but gone before
Has crossed the river, reached the shore
And from the eternal height look o'er
And beckons us to Heaven

ELLIOTT, Milford R. - 1891-1955.
  James - 1818-1896.
  Mary A. - his wife, 1819-1884.
  Joseph E. - 1851-1924.
  Ella M. - his wife, 1852-1927.
  Fred B. - 1857-1922.
  James H. - 1840 - died at sea 1864.

COOMBS, Josiah G. - son of John and Charlotte Coombs, born in Bowdoin 4 Aug 1804, died in New York, NY, 12 Jul 1854.
  Abigail - dau of Solomon & Peggy Eaton, wife of Josiah G Coombs, born in Bowdoin 25 Dec 1808, died in Bowdoinham 25 Nov 1875.
  Rowland L. E. - son of Josiah G and Abigail Coombs, born in Cincinnati O. 18 May 1831, died in Bowdoin 6 May 1834.
BLAKE, John R. - 25 Apr 1891-9 Feb 1970.

Marguerite I. - his wife, 1892-1944.
James F. - son of Reuben & Philena Blake, born in Bowdoinham 16 Mar 1836, died in Boston, Mass 24 Jul 1866.
Charlotte A. - dau of Josiah C. & Abigail Coombs, wife of James F. Blake, born in Bowdoinham 19 Sep 1833, died in Waterville 13 Oct 18<u>55</u> (death year on stone verified).
Willard E. - their son, born 19 Jul 18<u>56</u>, died 5 Apr 1922 (birth year on stone verified).
Lizzie M. - his wife, 29 May 1868, 5 Oct 1960.

DAVIS, Renton Perley - 1882-1944.
Charlivine B. - his wife, 1889-1954.

COOMBS, Rowland L. E. - son of Josiah C. and Abigail Coombs, born in Bowdoinham 21 Nov 1835, died in Bowdoinham 2 Feb 1867.
Mary H. - dau of Henry & Rachel Parker, wife of Rowland L. E. Coombs, born in Waltham, Mass 18 Aug 1842, died in Andover, Mass 28 Apr 1865.
John C. - son of Josiah C. & Abigail Coombs, born in Bowdoinham 8 Mar 1845, died in Boston, Mass. 7 Jan 1905.
Viola V. - dau of Josiah C. and Abigail Coombs born in Bowdoinham 6 Feb 1843, died in Portland 22 Apr 1934.

WOODBURY, David - 22 Mar 1823-21 Jul 1896.
Peggy R. - dau of Josiah C. & Abigail Coombs, wife of David Woodbury, born in Bowdoinham 21 Nov 1838, died in Wellesley, Mass. 26 Sep 1865.
D. Harold - son of David and Peggy R. Woodbury, born in South Natick, Mass. 19 Oct 1855, died in Bowdoinham 19 Oct 1856.
Freddie E. - son of David and Peggy R. Woodbury, born in Bowdoinham 2 Jan 1857, died South Natick, Mass. 29 Apr 1863.

BLAKE, John R. - Massachusetts 2nd Lieut Air SVC World War I, 25 Apr 1891-9 Feb 1970.

Nelson Family Lot - from the intersection of Routes 201 and 125, go 1.9 miles towards the Town of Richmond. Turn right into the drive of the former Maine Forest Service building. Walk in back of the building and turn right on woods road. Go approximately 200 feet, and the cemetery is on the left.

NELSON, Peter Captain - died 1 Mar 1874 at 61 yrs. 11 (?) m.
Hannah - wife of Peter Nelson, died 2 Oct 1896 at 79 yrs.
JORDAN, Anna M. - wife of James Jordan, died 22 Jul 1884 at 42 yrs.

Emery Purinton Farm Cemetery - from the intersection of Routes 201 and 125, go 2.8 miles towards the Town of Richmond. Turn left on the Adams Road. A short distance on this road at the left, you will find a culvert over which is a mowed road. The cemetery is in a couple of hundred feet. These inscriptions were copied 14 October 1972.

PURINTON, Sarah E. - dau of E. E. & H. M. Purinton, 1884-1909.
Gladys E. Knowlton - wife of Horace Purinton, 1892-1952.
Stephen - 1 or 7 Oct 1839-6 Jun 1907.
Alice M. - his wife, 24 Jan 1840-24 Dec 1906.
CLEVELAND, Emily Ann - dau of E. S. Cleveland, 14 Aug 1968.
PURINTON,   - (no marker; new grave in 1972 and probably that of the wife of Emery Purinton).
Emery E. - 1859-1929.
Hattie G. Rhoades - his wife, 1862-1942.

Roland E. - O M 1/C USN, son of Emery E. & Hattie M. Purinton, 1896-1918.
Sarah E. - dau of Emery & Hattie Purinton, 1884-1909.
Horace - son of Emery & Hattie Purinton, 188_-197_.
Emily - died Aug 1883 and was dau of Abel & Mary Purinton (no stone but information from family record).
Abiezer - died 8 Jun 1858 at 78 yrs. 8 m. 28 d.
Eunice, Mrs. - wife of Abiezer Purinton, died 26 Mar 1842 at 64 yrs. (family record says May).

Weep not when Christians die
Weep not when saints ascend
From weariness and woe
To God their heavenly Friend;
O rather sing when those we love
Have safely reached their home above.

ALLEN, Ernest L. - son of L. C. & M. R. Allen, died 19 Nov 1875 at 2 yrs. 2 m. 7 d.

Gem of our hearth
Our household pride
Earth's undefiled
Could love have saved thou
 hadst not died
Dear sweet child.

CRAWFORD, Maria Purinton - wife of Jas Crawford 1833-1894.
PURINTON, Mary Raymond - wife of Abel Purinton, 1804-1889.
Abel - 1806-1891.
Amos - father, 1813-1897.

Martha J. - wife of Amos Purinton, 1822-1906.
Frances E. - wife of Rev Cyrus Purinton, 1845-1897.
Cyrus, Rev. - died 28 Oct 1927 (no stone but date from family record).
Ida May - dau of Rev. E. & D. E. Purinton, died 1 Aug 1873 at 17 yrs. 4 m.
Elisha, Rev. - father, 1811-1880.
Deborah E. - mother, wife of Rev Elisha Purinton, 1814-1892.

Carr Cemetery - from the intersection of Routes 201 and 125, go on Route 201 2.2 miles to the Millay Road and turn right. Go about one mile, and the cemetery is on the right.

ADAMS, William O. - 1855-1929.
  Etta Conway - his wife, 1864-1928.
  Howard F. - 1903-1960.
  Nathan - died 13 Dec 1894 at 82 yrs.
  Durinda S. - his wife, died 29 Dec 1913 at 83 yrs.

  Oh my darling thy hast left us
  For a glorious home above
  With they Father gone before thee
  Singing praises to thy God.

  Robert - died 4 Nov 1905 at 44 yrs. 3 m.
CARR, Robert S. - 1856-1916.
  Theresa S. - his wife, 1859-
  William - 1819-1900.
  Ruth - his wife, 1821-
LUNT, Annie C. - died 6 Nov 1871 at 88 yrs. 2 m.
GODING, Clara A. - dau of Otis & Sarah S. Goding died 29 Oct 1859 at 11 m. 13 d.

Sarah A. - wife of Otis Goding, died 20 Feb 1862 at 24 yrs. 8 m.
STARBIRD, Sally - wife of Daniel Starbird, died 12 Aug 1864 at 64 yrs. 4 m. 16 d.

Dear wife and mother you have left us
While on earth was kind and true;
But we hope to meet you in heaven above
Where all is peace and joy and love.

Daniel, Capt. - died 12 Aug 1885 at 84 yrs. 6 m. 21 d.
Sarah - his wife, died 12 Aug 1864 at 64 yrs. 4 m. 15 d.
Robert S. - died 3 Aug 1863 at 35 yrs. 6 m.
Franklin - died 25 Sep 1844 at 2 yrs. 6 m.
Sarah Ann - died 20 Feb 1861 at 24 yrs. 8 m.
Daniel W.
Caroline.
Aurlyer.
Durinda S.   (no dates)
William H.
Joseph A.
Alonzo R.
Children of Capt. Daniel & Sarah Starbird.
Clara A. - dau of Alonzo R. and Vesta Starbird died 11 Feb 1861 at 1 yr. 1 m.
Vesta - wife of Alonzo R. Starbird, died 11 May 1861 at 21 yrs.
Alonzo R. - father, died 9 Mar 1909 at 70 yrs.
Margaret - mother, wife of Alonzo R. Starbird died 3 Dec 1904 at 60 yrs. 9 m.
Minnie L. - dau of Alonzo R. & Margaret Starbird, died 30 May 1894 at 25 yrs. 5 m.
George M. - son of A R & M Starbird, died 26 Jul 1865 at 2 yrs. 4 m.
Nellie A. - dau of Alonzo R & Margaret Starbird, died 1 Jan 1890 at 24 yrs. 6 m.

Frank J. - son of Alonzo R. & Margaret Starbird died 1 Dec 1905 at 26 yrs.
D. W. - Corp'l Co. F 19 ME Inf (there are no dates, but Bowdoin Selectmen's records show Daniel W Starbird 1822-2 Feb 1902).
Franklin - son of Robert S & Abby A Starbird, died 1 Oct 1851 at 10 m. 14 d.

JACK, Joseph - died 21 Sep 1873 at 65 yrs.

CARR, Joshua P. - father, 1816-1896.
Caroline R. - mother, wife of Joshua P. Carr, 1824-1915.
James T. - brother, 1850-1920.
Isaac - son of Joshua P & Caroline Carr, died 20 Aug 1847 at 1 yr. 7 m.
Isaac C. - son of Joshua P & Caroline S Carr, died 14 Apr 1869 at 21 yrs. 5 m.

None knew him but to love him.

Dear Son and Brother we give thee up,
And sorrowing drink the bitter cup.
But we hope to meet thee on that bright shore,
Where sorrows and parting will be no more.

Robert S. - son of J. P. & C. Carr, died 5 Apr 1855 at 1 yr. 5 m.
Sarah - dau of Nathaniel & Elvina Carr, died 20 Sep 1845.
Isaac - son of Joseph & Sarah Carr, died 28 Jun 1843 at 22 yrs.
Joseph - died 29 Nov 1860 at 72 yrs.
Sally - wife of Joseph Carr, died 27 Nov 1877 at 85 yrs.

WILSON, A. H. - husband, died 30 Dec 1874 at 35 yrs. 9 m.
Fannie E. - wife of A H Wilson, died 8 Jul 1870 at 26 yrs.

Ah Death! Thy summons is hard to bear;
Thou takest from Earth, the good and the
   fair;
Thou has left us here in sorrow to mourn
The loss of the loved and cherished one.

Can it be that the wealth of that fair
   white brow
Is moldering neath the earth's sod now
Has that lovely form no resting place
Save the chill dark grave and death's cold
   embrace.

We will meet her again in that world of
   love,
If we dwell on earth with our thoughts above.
When we reach that glorious celestial shore
We shall join the loved just gone before.

Oh! not perchance is the records of time
In glowing words is written her name
But shrined in each heart that loved her well
Her memory ever shall sacred dwell.

(Beside the stones of A. H. Wilson and Fannie
E. Wilson is a stone marked "Little Carrie.")

Cornish or Gully Woods Cemetery - from the intersection of Routes 201 and 125, go 1 mile towards Bowdoin Center. Just beyond the Bowdoin Central School, turn left into the first driveway. At the top of the hill and to the right is the cemetery.

BEAL, Benj. A. - father, died 26 Jan 1907 at
   79 yrs. 27 d.
   Sarah E. - mother, wife of Benj A Beal,
   died 23 Jul 1891 at 53 yrs. 8 m.

Nath'l - father, died 19 Jul 1884 at 84 yrs.
Mary - mother, his wife, died 30 Mar 1876 at
81 yrs. 9 m.
CROCKER, Lydia - wife of Samuel M Crocker,
died 25 Jun 1857 at 20 yrs. 3 m.
CORNISH, James - 1784-1844.
Charity - wife of James Cornish, died 16 Mar
1876 at 84 yrs.

Grace the guardian of our dust
Crown the treasury of the skies
Every atom of thy trust
Rest in hope again to rise.

Wm., Capt. - 1822-1904.
Eri B. - 1830-1844.
Susan A. Lewis - 1834-1890.
James - son James and Charity Cornish, died
20 Apr 1846 at 63 yrs (when we copied this
inscription, the top of the stone was broken
off, and we could not read the name, etc.,
but <u>Bowdoin Vital Records</u> show the informa-
tion we could not read).
Eri B. - son of James & Charity Cornish died
13 Oct 1846 at 16 yrs.
COOMBS, Margaret, Mrs. - wife of Joseph Coombs,
died 7 Apr 1836 at 33 yrs (stone states,
"Also, her infant").
Thomas - son of Joseph & Margaret Coombs,
died 29 Dec 1843 at 15 yrs.
Charlotte - 2nd wife of John Coombs, departed
this life 17 Nov 1844 at 71 yrs.
John, Capt. - departed this life 20 Apr 1836
at 88 yrs (Revolutionary marker).
SMALL, William O. - 24 Aug 1857-22 Jul 1910.
PARTON, Nelson - born 17 Jul 1853, died 7 Feb
1904.
Mary Orr Jacques - mother, wife of Thomas

Parton, 1820-1898.
CORNISH, Hattie S. - 1872-1883.
  David P. - 1828-1912.
  Mary E. - his wife, 1833-1878.

Thompson Cemetery - from the intersection of Routes 201 and 125, go 1.7 miles towards the Town of Topsham. Turn right on the Doughty Road. The cemetery is on the immediate left of the road. Some inscriptions not found by us have been taken from the <u>Bowdoin Vital Records</u>. We copied the inscriptions in 1991.

THOMPSON, Amos - 3 Sep 1749-6 Jun 1835 (Revolutionary soldier).
  Thomas (?) - died 6 Jan 1830 or 1880 at 86 yrs.
  Hannah, Mrs. - died 26 Jan 1835 at 84 yrs.
  Phineas - died 20 Nov 1860 at 89 yrs (<u>Bowdoin Vital Records</u>, husband Jemima, died 22 Nov 1860 at 80 yrs).
  Mary (Metcalf) - 2nd wife of Phineas Thompson, died 10 Dec 1819 at 33 yrs. 7 m.
  Jemima (Blake) - 3rd wife of Phineas Thompson, died Jun 1823 (not necessarily buried here).
  Mehetable - 1st wife of Phineas Thompson, died Sep 1804 (<u>Bowdoin Vital Records</u>, dau of Ebenezer and Martha (Smith) Preble of Woolwich - not necessarily buried here).
JAQUES, Mary, Mrs. - died 30 Nov 1822 at 56 yrs.
  Anna, Mrs. - died 2 Feb 1847 at 67 yrs.
  Wives of Isaac Jaques.
  Isaac - died 16 Oct 1847 at 82 yrs.

Rogers Family Cemetery – from the intersection of Routes 201 and 125, go 1/10th of a mile towards the Town of Richmond to the Rogers Homestead on the right. The cemetery is at the back of the house.

ROGERS, Mary, Mrs. – wife of James Rogers, Esq, died 6 Oct 1811 at 53 yrs.
  James – died 26 Feb 1835 at 78 yrs.
  Bertie – son of George & Mary J. Rogers, died 4 Apr 1879 at 13 yrs. 8 m.
  Viola G. – dau of George & Mary J Rogers, died 9 Dec 1862 at 5 yrs. 6 m.
  George E. – son of George & Mary J. Rogers, died 10 Mar 1862 at 10 m.
  Elizabeth J. – dau of George & Mary J Rogers, died 27 Jul 1904 at 53 yrs. 8 m.
  Jane – wife of George Rogers, died 22 Jul 1860 at 75 yrs.
  George – died 3 Jan 1860 at 73 yrs.
POWERS, Richard – died 30 Sep 1860 at 69 yrs.
ROGERS, George – father, died 7 Aug 1895 at 79 yrs.
  Mary J. – mother, wife of George Rogers, died 16 Nov 1899 at 74 yrs. 11 m.
  George – 1900-1936.
  Everette – 1868-1930.
  Mary E. – 1878-1942.
MERRIMAN, Harmon – (no dates).
  Viola A. Rogers – wife of Harmon Merriman, 29 Jan 1863-16 Feb 1911.

Bradford Haskell Cemetery – we have been unable to locate this cemetery in the Town of Bowdoin. According to the Bowdoin Selectmen's records, a 1st Lt. Thomas Berry is buried in this cemetery. This man served in the Revolutionary War in Captain Richard Mayberry's Company,

Colonel Francis' Regiment at Winter Hill, Boston, Dorchester Heights, having enlisted on 23 January 1776 at Brunswick, Maine. The <u>DAR</u> <u>Patriot</u> <u>Index</u> shows this man as being born in 1745, marrying Abigail Coombs, and dying 27 January 1828, a Massachusetts lieutenant (but we must remember that Maine until 1820 was a part of MA.) The <u>Bowdoin</u> <u>Vital</u> <u>Records</u> show a marriage on 16 February 1773 of Abigail Coombs, daughter of George and Abigail (Berry) Coombs, to Lieut. Thomas Berry, and the cross reference under Berry adds "resided in Portland."

Jack Cemetery - here again, we have been unable to locate this cemetery, but <u>Bowdoin</u> <u>Vital</u> <u>Records</u> indicate it is in North Bowdoin. Bowdoin Selectmen's records show Andrew Jack, 3rd being buried in this cemetery, and that he was born 1776 and died 4 August 1844, having enlisted at Bowdoin 20 Jun 1814 and being discharged 28 Sep 1814 (presumbably for the War of 1812). He served at Bath in Captain N. McLellan's Company, Lt. Colonel Merrill's Regiment. <u>Bowdoin</u> <u>Vital</u> <u>Records</u> state that Andrew was the husband of Betsy Weymouth, and that there was no issue. According to the <u>Bowdoin</u> <u>Vital</u> <u>Records</u>, the following are also buried in the Jack Cemetery.

JACK, Joseph, Capt. - husband Mary (Gray), died 1 Sep 1833.
  Mary (Gray) - 2nd wife Capt. Joseph Jack, d. 4 Mar 1854.

Potter Cemetery - this burial ground is located in the Town of Lisbon Falls (once a part of the Town of Bowdoin), but is being included as some persons buried there were early Bowdoin residents. To reach the cemetery, go 3.2 miles from the intersection of Routes 196 and 125 in Lisbon Falls. Turn left at the West Road and at the bottom of the hill, bear left onto Bowdoinham Road. Go about 1/4 mile and turn left on the Rabbit Road and follow down stream to the left of the road. The cemetery is on a high wooded knoll overlooking the brook. This burial lot is in extremely bad condition with many stones completely shattered, some buried under several inches of soil, and probably some stones are completely gone.

SMULLEN, John - died 21 Jul 1825 at 60 yrs.
  Bethiah - wife of John Smullen, died 2 Feb 1847 at 84 yrs.
  Mary - wife of John Smullen, died 17 Jul 1806 at 38 yrs.
  Martha - dau of John & Mary Smullen, died 9 Feb 1806 at 13 yrs.
  William - son of John and Mary Smullen, died 23 Mar 1806 at 1 m.11d.
  Joseph D. - died 26 Feb 1869 at 72 yrs. 10 m.
  Rachel - wife of Joseph D Smullen, died 23 Aug 1853 at 49 yrs.
  Thomas W. - son of Joseph D & Rachel H Smullen died 30 Dec 1837 at 18 m.
  (There is a small field stone.)
TIBBETTS, Phebe - wife of Thomas Tibbetts, died 2   1859 (month not readable), at 95 yrs.
  Thomas, Mr. - died 7 Oct 184? at 73 yrs.
  Samuel, Deacon - died 22 Dec 1870 at 74 yrs.
  Hannah - wife of Samuel Tibbetts, died 13 Feb 1857 at 59 yrs. 6 m.

SAWYER, Sarah M. - wife of George Sawyer, a dau of Dea Samuel & Hannah Tibbetts, died 18 Mar 18 (?) at 18 yrs. 8 m.

TIBBETTS, Rachel - dau of Hannah & Samuel Tibbetts, died 14 Oct 18 (?) at 26 yrs.

KIMBALL, John, Mr. - died 31 ___ 1838 (month of death and age not readable).

EATON, Abner, Mr. - died 10 Sep 1844 at 54 yrs.

Precious in the sight of the Lord is the death of <u>his</u> Saints.

Hannah D., Mrs. - wife of Abner Eaton, died 15 Oct 1844 at 51 yrs.

Day Burial Lot - we have been unable to locate this burial lot, but <u>Bowdoin Vital Records</u> state it is in North Bowdoin and shows the following persons as being buried there.

DAY, Jotham, Rev. - husband of Mary Ann, died 11 Mar 1862 at 81 yrs. 8 m.
Mary Ann - wife of Rev Jotham Day, died 31 Aug 1841 at 61 yrs. 6 m. in Webster.

REVOLUTIONARY WAR VETERANS

Many of Bowdoin's early settlers were Revolutionary War veterans, but incomplete records make it impossible to name them all. Information in this list has been taken from cemetery inscriptions, Bowdoin Selectmen's records, <u>Bowdoin Vital Records</u>, compiled by Rachel Townsend Cox, and from various family records, as well as from <u>An Alphabetical Index of Revolutionary Pensioners Living in Maine</u> by Charles Flagg, and the <u>DAR Patriot Index</u> (6th Printing, 1979), and supplements thereto. The service records for many of these men are recorded in the <u>Massachusetts Soldiers and Sailors of the Revolutionary War</u>, compiled from the Archives and prepared and published by the Secretary of the Commonwealth (1896-1908).

ADAMS, Samuel, b. 1757/8; d. 20 Aug 1840 at 83 yrs; m. (1) Hannah Buker; (2) Elizabeth Gardner.
ADAMS, Thomas; m. Sarah Tarr.
ALLEN, Daniel, b. 1 May 1760; d. 4 Oct 1842 at 81 yrs; m. Margaret (Margery) Coombs.
ALLEN, John, 2nd, b. 14 Apr 1767; d. 14 Jul 1820.
BERRY, Thomas, b. 1845; d. 27 Jan 1828; m. 16 Feb 1773, Abigail Coombs.
BOOKER, Daniel, b. 25 Feb 1760; d. 8 Nov 1856 at 97 yrs; m. Mary Douglass.
BRIMINGION, Thomas, b. 1754; d. 17 Dec 1843 at 89 yrs; m. Ruth .
BUBIER, Joseph, b. 17 Jul 1728; d. aft 1781; m. (1) Phebe (?)   ; (2) Martha Grover.
CHASE, Isaac, b. 1760; d. 6 Feb 1842 at 82 yrs.

COOMBS, John, b. 1 Nov 1748; d. 20 Apr 1836 at 88 yrs; m. (1) Savia Brown; (2) Charlotte Tarr (DAR Patriot Index says b. 11 Nov 1748).

DENNETT, John, b. 28 Jun 1767; d. 27 Nov 1843 at 76 yrs; m. 24 Nov 1802, Anna Starbird.

DOYLE, Michael, b. 1760; d. 1846.

FERRIN, Richard, b. 1759; d. 1845; m. Ruth

FREEZE, John; m. Sarah   (as a widow she m. a Card).

GILPATRICK, Nathaniel, b. ab 1749; d. 30 May 1834 at 85 yrs; m. Abigail Higgins.

HALL, Luther, d. Oct 1826 at 74 yrs.

JENKINS, Lemuel, b. ab 1752; d. aft 1836 (<u>Bowdoin Vital Records</u>, 1835 at 72 yrs); m. 29 Aug 1775, Abigail Shepard.

MITCHELL, Samuel.

POTTER, James, b. 1734; d. 22 Mar 1815 at 81 yrs; m. 5 Dec 1759, Mary Spear.

POTTER, James, Jr.; m. (1) Hannah   ; (2) Susannah

PURINTON, Humphrey, b. 16 Aug 1759; d. 28 Jan 1832 at 73 yrs; m. Thankful Snow.

PURINTON, Nathaniel, b. 23 Oct 1756; d. 13 Jun 1832; m. Hipsibeth Snow.

RANDALL, Hatherly, Capt., b. ab 1766; d. 19 Apr 1858 at 92 yrs. 7 m. 23 d; m. Elizabeth

RANDALL, Joseph, b. 1755; d. 7 Aug 1818 at 63 yrs; m. (int) 6 Apr 1778, Martha Reed.

RIDEOUT, Stephen, b. 1760; d. 15 Sep 1843; m. (1) Abigail ("Nabby") Smart; (2) 16 Aug 1807, Jane Works.

RIDLEY, Daniel, b. 4 Apr 1759; d. 1 Apr 1837; m. 27 Nov 1781, Hannah Bridges.

RIDLEY, George, b. 1761; d. 31 Oct 1818; m. Mary ("Molly") Hopkins.

SMALL (SMALLEY), David, b. 1 Jan 1750; d. 17 Jul 1811; m. (1) Elizabeth   ;

(2) 2 May 1780, Dorcas Parlin (<u>DAR</u> <u>Patriot</u> <u>Index</u> gives b. as 27 Jan 1750).

SMALL, Ephraim, b. 1759/60; d. 8 Jan 1842; m. Dorcas Ccombs.

SMALL, Joseph, b. 24 Aug 1748; d. 13 Feb 1831; m. Mindwell Purington.

SNOW, Joshua, b. Apr 1760; d. 24 Apr 1839 at 79 yrs; m. (1) Molly Roberts; (2) Sarah Harpswell.

STARBIRD, Samuel, b. 1758; d. 1 Sep 1839; m. Alicia Elsey.

TARR, Joseph, b. 1759; d. 4 Jan 1845; m. Deborah Toothaker.

TEMPLE, John, Lt., b. 7 Oct 1756; d. 13 Jan 1842 at 85 yrs; m. Mary Mason.

THOMPSON, Amos, b. 3 Sep 1749; d. 6 Jun 1835 at 86 yrs; m. Hannah Wooster.

VARNEY, Ichabod; son of Timothy & Joanna (Hanson) Varney; prob. b. Dover, NH; resided Bowdoin.

WHITNEY, Ebenezer; m. Mehitable   ; removed from Brunswick to Litchfield bef 1800; then to Bowdoin where a son was b.

WILLIAMS, George, b. ab 1752/4; d. 1825; m. (1) Grace Adams; (2) Mary ("Polly") Totman.

WILLIAMS, Jonathan, bap. 12 Jun 1763; d. ab 1791; m. Rachel Ridley.

WILSON, Joseph.

WAR OF 1812 VETERANS

This list has been compiled from cemetery inscriptions and from Bowdoin Selectmen's records. It is probably incomplete.

ADAMS, David A., b. Oct 1800; d. 15 Mar 1839 at 37 yrs. 5 m.
ADAMS, Samuel, b. 20 Jan 1802; d. 10 Nov 1882 at 80 yrs. 9 m. 10 d.
ALEXANDER, James, b. 1787; d. 21 Jul 1857 at 72 yrs.
ANDREWS, William; d. 4 May 1868 at 78 yrs.
BATCHELDER, Samuel E., b. 25 Feb 1781; d. 8 Nov 1863 at 82 yrs. 8 m. 13 d.
BUBIER, Mark.
COOMBS, Zebulon, b. 20 Mar 1780; d. 12 Apr 1850.
FLAGG, William E., b. 27 Aug 1843; d. 11 May 1892.
GROVER, James, b. 1802; d. 26 Mar 1859 at 57 yrs.
HALL, Martin, b. 12 Aug 1787; d. 11 Feb 1861.
HANSCOM, Samuel, b. 1778; d. 24 Aug 1851 at 73 yrs. 3 m.
HIGGINS, Jeremiah, Capt., b. 25 Feb 1786; d. 25 Jul 1867 at 81 yrs. 5 m.
JACK, Andrew, 3rd, b. 1776; d. 4 Aug 1844.
KNIGHT, Daniel; d. 11 Sep 1858 at 81 yrs.
MAXWELL, Solomon, b. 26 Jan 1781; d. 26 Dec 1868 at 87 yrs. 6 m. 22 d.
NICHOLS, Benjamin, b. 20 Jan 1780; d. 6 Mar 1859.
NILES, Frederick, b. 1799; d. 1869.
PATTERSON, Elisha, Col., b. 1794; d. 19 May 1860 at 66 yrs.
OLIVER, John, b. 1768; d. 21 Sep 1848 at 80 yrs.
RANKS, John, b. 14 Feb 1776; d. 28 May 1867 at 91 yrs.
RIDLEY, Ruben; lost at sea from Privateer <u>Dash</u>.

RIDLEY, William, b. 1783; d. 14 Oct 1860 at 77 yrs. 8 m.
SMALL, Elisha, b. 1800; d. 17 Feb 1872 at 73 yrs. 2 m.
SNOW, Moses, b. 1794; d. 26 Apr 1884 at 89 yrs. 7 m.
STARBIRD, Daniel, Capt., b. 21 Jan 1801; d. 12 Aug 1885 at 84 yrs. 6 m. 21 d.
STARBIRD, William H.
TEMPLE, Ivory; d. 9 Sep 1852 at 45 yrs. 4 m.
TOWNSEND, Benjamin, b. 1800; d. 1870.
WHITE, Gideon, b. 1794; d. 9 Nov 1836 at 42 yrs.
WHITE, Isaac, b. 1803; d. 6 Apr 1864 at 61 yrs.
WHITE, Isaac, b. 1771; d. 1 Sep 1858 at 87 yrs.

CIVIL WAR VETERANS

The monument at Bowdoin Center, dedicated in 1907, lists the names of 127 men who went to war. The following enumeration includes these names and also the names of Bowdoin men extracted from cards which were made from the Civil War Muster Rolls at the Maine State Archives, as well as all names found in Bowdoin cemetery inscriptions and on GAR markers which referred to Civil War service. Additionally, information set forth below has been taken from Bowdoin Selectmen's records and from the <u>Bowdoin Vital Records</u> compiled by Rachel Townsend Cox. These sources reveal that at least 187 Civil War veterans were associated with the Town of Bowdoin, although possibly in a few cases they did not live in Bowdoin but were only buried in the town, and some, of course, such as John Libby Bickford, who was killed at the Battle of the Wilderness, never returned home.

ADAMS, Daniel R., b. Nov 1814; d. 26 Sep 1888.
ADAMS, Isaac R.
ADAMS, John B.
ADERTON, Jerry M.
ALDERSON, James.
ALEXANDER, James E.
ALEXANDER, John L., b. 1843; d. 1928.
ALLEN, Elijah, Jr.
ALLEN, Henry R.
ALLEN, Isaac.
ALLEN, Ivory T., b. 4 Feb 1836; d. 26 May 1909.
ALLEN, Thomas S.
ALLEN, William C., b. Jan 1838; d. 22 Sep 1875 at 37 yrs. 8 m.
ANDERSON, Zacheus (Zachariah).

APPLEBY, Levi A., b. 1840; d. 1919.
BEAL, Benj. A., b. ab 1827; d. 26 Jan 1907 at 79 yrs. 27 d.
BEAL, Nathaniel A., b. 1830; d. 24 Apr 1908 at 78 yrs.
BENSON, James D.
BERRY, Reed.
BIBBER, Benjamin P.; d. 19 Aug 1915 at 72 yrs. 4 m.
BICKFORD, John L., b. 1843; killed Battle of the Wilderness 6 May 1864 at 21 yrs.
BICKFORD, Levi, b. 1836; d. 11 Oct 1903.
BLANCHARD, Loyel, b. Sep 1809; d. 9 May 1883 at 73 yrs. 8 m.
BOOBIER, Artemus W., b. Jul 1842; d. 10 Sep 1880 at 38 yrs. 2 m. 19 d.
BOOBIER, Daniel.
BOOKER, Elisha.
BOOKER, Israel, Jr.; killed in action 7 Jun 1864.
BOWIE, James H.
BROWN, Daniel S.
BROWN, Joseph F., Capt., b. 22 Jan 1835; d. 16 Jun 1906.
BUKER, Charles.
BUKER, George W., b. Aug 1837; d. 28 Jun 1863 at 25 yrs. 10 m.
BUKER, Joseph E.
BUKER, Orrington L.
BUKER, Wm. G., Jr., b. 14 Feb 1834; d. 3 Jul 1912.
CAMPBELL, Abial.
CAMPBELL, Albion H., b. 1 Dec 1823; d. 3 Apr 1897.
CAMPBELL, George Jackson; d. 23 Sep 1862 at Culpepper, VA.
CARR, Thomas H.
CARTER, Edwin.
CARTER, Joseph S., b. Mar 1848; d. 14 Sep 1864 at 16 yrs. 6 m.

CARTER, William S., b. 29 May 1846; d. 22 Jan 1892 at 45 yrs.
CHASE, David.
CHRISTOPHER, John E.
COLBY, Otis R., Lt., b. 6 Aug 1834; d. 13 Jun 1865.
COOMBS, Charles.
COOMBS, Francis B., b. 13 Sep 1847; d. 25 Dec 1929.
COOMBS, Frank B.
COOMBS, Israel A., b. 1836; d. 1891.
COOMBS, James H.; d. 25 Apr 1864 at 17 yrs.
COOMBS, James, Jr., b. 1826; d. 14 Aug 1864, at Baton Rouge, LA.
COOMBS, Rowland L. E., 2nd, b. 21 Nov 1835; d. 2 Feb 1867.
COOMBS, Samuel Pierce.
CORNISH, David P., b. 1828; d. 12 Jul 1912.
COTTON, William S., Col., d. 13 Apr 1888 at 72 yrs. 9 m. 8 d.
CURTIS, Henry, b. 22 May 1834; d. 31 Dec 1862 at 28 yrs. 7 m. 9 d.
CURTIS, George S.
CURTIS, Nehemiah, b. 1838; d. 4 Oct 1925.
DANFORTH, Hartwell.
DANFORTH, Levi.
DENNETT, Charles.
DENNETT, Menander.
DENNETT, Moses S.; killed in action Battle of the Wilderness.
DOUGLAS, Edwin C.
DOYLE, Charles H., b. 1846; d. 20 Sep 1918.
DOYLE, George E.
DOYLE, Johnson J., b. 1844; d. 5 Oct 1910.
DUNN, William, b. 28 Apr 1834; d. 18 Mar 1902; received Congressional Medal of Honor.
DYER, Elbridge.
EMERSON, William J., b. 4 Sep 1837; d. 25 Jun 1898.

FREEMAN, Albion K. P.
FRENCH, Howard (bur. Hix Small Cem., no stone).
FULLER, Seth.
GARDINER, Charles C., b. 1842; d. 31 Aug 1861 at 19 yrs.
GARDINER, John L.
GLIDDEN, George.
GOULD, Harris (Harrison) A.
GROVER, Boynton.
GROVER, Jordan.
GROVER, King T., b. 1835; d. 10 Mar 1875 at 40 yrs. 2 m.
GROVER, John C., b. Jun 1846; d. Lynn, MA, 9 Oct 1865 at 19 yrs. 4 m.
GROVER, Winfield N., b. 1855; d. 10 Mar 1879 at 24 yrs.
HAYNES, James D.; d. 1 Jun 1863 at Bonnet Carre, LA.
HAYNES, Winfield S.
HIGGINS, B. Franklin; d. 1865 (bur. W. Bowdoin Cem., no stone).
HIGGINS, Hiram, b. 1812; d. 14 Mar 1867 at 55 yrs.
HIGGINS, James C., b. 1841; d. 3 May 1863 at 22 yrs.
HIGGINS, John L.
HINE, Erastus Walton, killed in Battle of the Wilderness on his 27th birthday, 5 May 1864.
HOLBROOK, Charles H., b. 16 Aug 1848; d. 15 Aug 1920.
JONES, Lewis.
O'KEEFE, Jeremiah, b. 3 Mar 1845; d. 21 Mar 1909 (bur. Hix Small Cem., no stone).
KENNEDY, John.
KNIGHT, William J.
LEONARD, Melvin S., b. 1845; d. 20 Oct 1862 at New Orleans, LA.
LEONARD, Seth H., Capt., b. 1821; d. 1886.

LEWIS, Daniel W.
LEWIS, James C.
LEWIS, Joseph E., b. 1844; d. 17 Feb 1904.
MALOON, Horton, b. 1843; d. 16 Jul 1863 at 20 yrs. 5 m. 25 d. in battle near Shepardstown, VA.
MALOON, Samuel; d. 18 Oct 1862, Pensacola, FLA.
MALOON, William, Jr.
MARR, Edward, b. 18 Aug 1839; d. 24 Dec 1891.
MARR, Sidney, b. 1837; d. 1864 at Richmond, VA.
MARR, Winter, b. 1813; d. 15 Dec 1889 at 76 yrs.
MARRINER, Charles C.
MARSHALL, Mason H., b. 1835; d. 19 Nov 1895.
MAXWELL, Erastus W.
MAXWELL, Isaac L.
MAXWELL, Rufus S.
MAXWELL, William.
MEADER, Ancil (Ansel) D.; d. 3 Jan 1865; bur. at Barrancas, FLA.
MEADER, Clark; d. in hospital 20 Oct 1864.
MERRIMAN, David C.
MOUNTFORT, Albert.
MOUNTFORT, George W.
MOUNTFORT, Vincent; killed in action 16 Sep 1864.
MOUNTFORT, William.
MUDGE, Charles R., Lt. Col.; bur. W. Bowdoin Cem. on lot of Horatio Small.
MUNOY, Andrew C.
NELSON, Charles C.
NELSON, Peter, 2nd.
NILES, William, b. Jun 1835; d. at Matagorda, TX, 29 Dec 1863 at 23 yrs. 3 m.
O'GRADY, James, b. Rouses Point, Lake Champlain, NY, 2 Aug 1850 (no d. of death).

PATTERSON, Joseph R., Jr., b. May 1844; d. 2 Jan 1863 at 18 yrs. 8 m.
POLLEY, Thomas J.
POLLEY, Timothy H.; discharged and d. Baton Rouge, LA, 2 Aug 1863.
POTTER, James P.
PRESTON, Charles, b. 23 Feb 1826; d. 4 Jul 1892.
PROUT, Lendall A., b. 15 Oct 1848; d. 25 Mar 1924.
PURINTON, Alonzo, b. 20 Sep 1847; d. 24 Aug 1916.
PURINTON, Nathaniel S., b. 24 Feb 1844; d. 1 Jun 1908.
PURINTON, Granville, b. 1836; d. 1885.
RIDLEY, Alexander, b. 24 Jun 1827; d. 18 Jan 1916.
RIDLEY, Ambrose C.
RIDLEY, Clark; starved to death in Andersonville Prison.
RIDLEY, Humphrey P., b. 1826; d. 4 Oct 1883 at 57 yrs.
RIDLEY, Thomas R.
RING, Isaac B., b. 6 Aug 1834; d. 20 Feb 1914.
RIVERS, Joseph.
ROGER, Alonzo, b. 1816; d. 7 Nov 1878.
ROGERS, Alpheus W.
ROGERS, Alphonso (Alfonso) P.
ROSS, Actor, b. 1820; d. 1865.
ROSS, Walter E.
SHAW, Thomas, Jr., b. 1832; d. 20 Feb 1914.
SMALL, Ephraim, 3rd.
SMALL, Horatio G., b. 16 Jul 1833; d. 6 Apr 1888.
SMALL, Joel, b. 10 Jul 1837; d. 29 Nov 1900.
SMALL, Joseph, b. 10 May 1844; d. 17 Jul 1923.
SMALL, Joshua.
SMALL, Simeon F.
SMALL, William H. H.

SMALL, Zacheus, Jr.
STARBIRD, Alonzo R., b. 1839; d. 9 Mar 1909, at 70 yrs.
STARBIRD, Daniel W., b. 1822; d. 2 Feb 1902.
STARBIRD, Isaac, b. 1811; d. 7 Sep 1883 at 72 yrs. 10 m. 17 d.
STARBIRD, Rufus S.; prisoner of war.
STEELE, John O.; taken prisoner at Stony Creek 29 Jun 1864.
STEWART, Sylvester; was prisoner of war; d. 9 Feb 1917.
SUTHERLAND, James S.
TARR, Alonzo L., b. 3 Jan 1843; d. 17 Feb 1917.
TARR, Daniel M., b. 24 Feb 1824; d. 30 Nov 1874 at 50 yrs. 9 m. 6 d.
TARR, Edwin O.
TARR, John B.
TARR, Lorenzo M.; d. 5 Feb 1863 at Fortress Monroe, VA of fever.
THOMPSON, William H.; d. 6 Oct 1863 at 19 yrs.
TOWNSEND, John.
TOWNSEND, Obediah R.
TRUFANT, William B., b. 3 Aug 1830; d. 3 Jun 1905.
VARNEY, Hiram, Jr., b. 19 Nov 1839; d. Washington, DC, 16 Jun 1862 at 22 yrs. 6 m. 27 d.
VARNEY, Zacheus, b. 14 Mar 1830; d. 14 Nov 1909.
VARNUM, Isaac, Sr.
WARD, George.
WARD, Joseph.
WHEELER, Actor; d. 8 Jan 1885 at 50 yrs. 7 m. 14 d.
WHITE, Charles, b. 1818; d. 6 Oct 1873 at 55 yrs.
WHITING, James.
WILLIAMS, Henry H., b. 18 Mar 1839; d. 11 Oct 1896.

WILLIAMS, Henry H., b. 18 Mar 1839; d. 11 Oct 1896.
WILLIAMS, Otis, b. 1820; d. 1890.
WILLIAMS, Stephen, b. 1821; d. 12 Oct 1893 at 72 yrs.
WILSON, A. H., b. Mar 1839; d. 30 Dec 1874 at 35 yrs. 9 m.
WILSON, Charles E.
WILSON, Henry M.
WILSON, William M.; d. Fortress Monroe, VA, 10 Feb 1863, fever.
WOODWORTH, Joseph, b. 1842; missing in action 11 Jul 1863.

ADDENDUM

<u>South Cemetery</u>

CARR, John - died 6 Feb 1872 at 76 yrs. 11 m. 23 d.
  Polly - his wife, died 7 Jun 1832 at 34 yrs.
  Julia A. - wife of John Carr, died 7 Apr 1879 at 68 yrs.

  Mother we lift the tearful eye
  To hear you calling from the sky
  O, how could we your absence bear
  But that the hope to meet you there.

  Rachel A. - died 23 Sep 1837 at 3 yrs. 6 m.
  Hannah - died 2 Dec 1841 at 6 yrs. 2 m.
  Martha - died 8 Aug 1853 at 3 yrs. 9 m.
  Children of John & Julia A. Carr.
  Artemas S. - died 9 Nov 1823 at 2 yrs. 3 m.
  Harriet - died 7 Jun 1832 at 6 yrs. 6 m.
  Children of John & Polly Carr.
HALL, John, Mr. - died 18 Sep 1834.
  Cynthia P., Miss - dau of Mr John & Mrs Tabitha Hall, died 18 Oct 1834 at 19 yrs.

  So fades the lovely blooming flower
  Frail smiling solace of an hour
  So soon our transient comforts fly
  And pleasure only blooms to die.

PLUMER, Jane W. - wife of Albert Plumer, died 8 Oct 1840 at 22 yrs.
HALL, Mary P. - wife of Albert Hall, died 5 Feb 1860 at 35 yrs. 11 m. 5 d.
  (There is a KP flag and room for a stone next to Mary, but no stone.)
  Edwin - son of A. & M. Hall, died 19 Sep 1851.

WILSON, Actor - 1777-1846.
  Apphia - 1779-1853.
  Stephen P. - 1819-1904.
  Maria A. - 1819-1902.
  Freddie - 1854-1856.
  William - 1846-1865.
  Melville - 1853-1941.
  Etta V. - his wife, 1861-1940.
WOODWORTH, Nathan - 1814-1890.
  Mercy Stover - his wife, 1816-1914.
  Joseph F. - 1842-1863 - a soldier of 1861.
  Emma A. - 1845-1868.
  Joseph - 1781-1842.
  Betsey - 1785-1853.
STOVER, Alcot, Esq. - died 6 Sep 1848 at 75 yrs. 6 m.
  Hannah - wife of Alcot Stover, died Jan 1876 at 98 yrs.
HALL, Levina J. - born 24 Feb 1830, died 21 Jul 1882.
  William - born 15 Jan 1820, died 2 Dec 1847.
  John B. - born 27 Oct 1826, died 15 Feb 1827.
  Martin - born 10 Aug 1787, died 11 Feb 1861.
  Jane - born 11 Apr 1792, died 19 May 1827.
  Elizabeth - born 6 Jan 1792, died 6 Nov 1876.
  Susan - born 21 Aug 1811, died 18 May 1833.
  Catharine - born 29 Nov 1812, died 19 May 1840.
  Thomas D. - born 29 Nov 1814, died 31 Aug 1837.
BIBBER, John - died 18 Dec 1851 at 68 yrs.
  Jane D. - wife of John Bibber, died 16 Mar 1872 at 84 yrs. 7 m.
  Ruth - died 19 Apr 1849 at 91 yrs. 5 m.
DOYLE, Huldah - wife of Jotham Doyle, died 3 Dec 1849 at 85 yrs. 26 d.
  Jotham - died 2 Nov 1788 at 28 yrs.

LEONARD, Huldah - mother, wife of James R.
  Leonard, died 5 Feb 1880 at 72 yrs.
MITCHELL, Hannah - wife of Robert E. Mitchell,
  died 17 Jan 1904 at 71 yrs.
POTTER, George, Mr. - died 9 Feb 1832 at 66
  yrs.
  Elizabeth - wife of George Potter, died 7
  Aug 1846 at 75 yrs.
  Phebe - dau of George & Elizabeth Potter,
  died 21 Mar 1845 at 36 yrs. 9 m.
  Emeline - dau of George & Elizabeth Potter,
  died 6 Oct 1849 at 35 yrs. 8 m 16 d.
BLANCHARD, Benjamin F. - 12 Jul 1859-9 Feb
  1919.
  Ida M. Trufant - his wife, 13 Jun 1861-
  Loyal B. - their son, 10 Jan 1897-13 Dec
  1913.
ZAUNSKI, Walter - 1884-1961 (funeral home
  marker).
PIERCE, Margaret D. - wife of Franklin Pierce,
  1 Oct 1883-29 Jun 1905 (dau of Benjamin &
  Ida Blanchard).
ALEXANDER, Chas. - died 15 Jun 1859 at 62 yrs.
  2 m.

  My heavenly home is bright and fair
  No sin nor death can enter there
  Its glittering towers the sun outshine
  That heavenly mansion now is mine.

  Bethiah L. - wife of Charles Alexander,
  died 21 Jul 1876 at 75 yrs. 10 m. 21 d.
  Betsey H. - died 8 Feb 1883 at 56 yrs. 4 m.
  Catherine - died 24 Jun 1888 at 96 yrs. 3 m.
BATCHELLOR, Lydia - wife of Nehemiah
  Batchellor, died 20 Nov 1858 at 64 yrs.
  Joseph C. - died 11 Jul 1861 at 35 yrs. 1 m.

Husband, Parent, Friend
Thou'rt gone from earth away
We waited at thy dying couch
But oh thy couldst not stay.

Be ye also ready, for in such an hour as
   ye think not the Son of Man cometh.

Fannie H. - wife of Jos. C. Batchellor, died
3 Nov 1856 at 22 yrs. 3 m, and their child
aged 6 wks.
John S. - died 1 Aug 1880 at 54 yrs. 2 m. 16 d.
CARR, Samuel (probably - top broken from stone)
died 1 Oct 1864 at 59 yrs. 15 d.
Thankful - wife of Samuel Carr, died 6 Aug
1880 at 73 yrs.
Josephine - dau of Samuel & Thankful Carr,
died 20 May 1868 at 28 yrs. 1 m. 14 d.

Living no longer yet living forever
In the purer light of the spiritual sun,
No dark stain of sin, no anguish can sever,
From the Father of Love our glorified one,
The light of our home unto Thee we resign,
They will be done, Father, Thy will and not
   mine.

HALL, Frankie B. - (on top of stone "Our Dar-
ling"), son of James M & Susan R Hall, died
27 Jul 1864 at 7 yrs. 4 m.
James M. - ("My Husband" on stone), died 22
Sep 1874 at 44 yrs. 10 m.
CARR, Horace G. - husband, father, born 14 Nov
1828, died 25 Apr 1879.
Susan Ellen Card - mother, wife of Horace G
Carr, born 16 Feb 1837, died 23 Mar 1911.
Emma M. - dau of Horace G and Susan E Carr,
died 15 Nov 1871 at 1 yr. 7 m. 8 d.

Emma May - dau of Horace G. & Susan E Carr, died 9 Feb 1877 at 5 yrs. 2 m.

ALEXANDER, William - died 28 Jul 1872 at 66 yrs. 3 m 19 d.
Nancie H. - wife of Wm. Alexander, died 18 Dec 1893 at 74 yrs. 8 m.

BLAKE, Mabel F. - dau of John F. & Rebecca S Blake, died 24 Oct 1883 at 23 yrs. 8 m.
Rebecca S. - wife of John F. Blake, died 28 Oct 1892 at 54 yrs. 2 m.
John F. - died 9 May 1910 at 78 yrs. 6 m.

BRADLEY, Willie S. - died 30 Oct 1860 at 4 yrs. 3 m.
Cori - died 16 Feb 1864 at 3 yrs. 2 m.
Children of C. E. & A. Bradley.
Charles E. - died 1 Feb 1903 at 86 yrs.
Adeline - his wife, died 20 Dec 1890 at 60 yrs. 7 m.

MARSHALL, Leon O. - 1895-1977.
Marjorie E. Strout - his wife, 1895-1980.
Harold E. - 10 Mar 1934-22 Nov 1989.
Ida M. - 15 Feb 1934-

CURTIS, John - 1826-1906.
Paulina Hall - 1832-1903.
Mehitable - mother, wife of Ezekiel Curtis, died 26 Mar 1882 at 81 yrs.
Ezekiel - father, died 24 Apr 1881 at 85 yrs.
Andrew - 1830-1832   )Children of Ezekiel
Hannah E. - 1838-1842)   and
Becca J. - 1841-1860)Mehitable Curtis.

TRUFANT, Adam - died 4 Oct 1855 at 54 yrs.
Marium (as spelled on stone) - wife of Adam Trufant, died 1 May 1845 at 45 yrs.

MOSELEY, Phineas T. - died 26 Jan 1891 at 75 yrs. 11 m. 14 d.
Charity - wife of P T Mosely, died 3 Feb 1881 at 64 yrs. 3 m. 10 d.

Clara E. - dau of P. T. and C. Mosely, died 5 Jul 1877 at 23 yrs. 9 m.
Alice D. - second dau of P. T. and Charity Mosely, died 4 Apr 1856 at 12 yrs. 8 m.
Orlando - son of P. T. and Charity Moseley, died 16 Sep 1851 at 4 yrs. 6 m.
Beulah - wife of Wm. Mosely, died 15 Jan 1872 at 83 yrs. 10 m.
William Mosely - died 11 Jul 1866 at 92 yrs.
Amos - son of Wm. & Bulah Mosely, died 15 Feb 1850.
Susan P. - dau of William & Beulah Moseley, died 27 Jan 1854 at 30 yrs.
Adelia C. - dau of Wm & Beulah Moseley, died 18 Dec 1870 at 41 yrs. 10 m.

BIBBER, Frank Edgar - born 3 Nov 1859, died 20 Mar 1936.
Alma Berttina - born 21 May 1855, died 7 Apr 1937.
Son and daughter of Martin H. and Charity Bibber.
William Alphonso - son of Martin H. and Charity C. Bibber, died 20 Sep 1851 at 22 m.
Charity C. - wife of Martin H. Bibber, 10 Mar 1826-24 May 1903.
Martin H. - 23 Nov 1823-8 Feb 1898.

HOGAN, William - died 25 Dec 1828 at 37 yrs. Erected by his sons 1856.

GROVER, Elizabeth - wife of Jonathan Grover, died 21 Oct 1849 at 52 yrs. 7 m.
(There is a broken, illegible stone.)
Lucy Jane - wife of Jonathan Grover, died 19 Dec 1850 at 24 yrs. 9 m.
Albert - my brother, died 14 Jan 1863 at 30 yrs.
Ruth - mother, wife of Bowdoin Grover, died 13 Jul 1878 at 75 yrs.
Bowdoin - father, died 27 May 1849 at 46 yrs.

   John C. - died in Lynn, MA, 9 Oct 1865 at 19 yrs. 4 m (GAR marker).
   Jeremiah M. - 1842-1907.
   Kate P. - his wife, 1832-   .
LANE, Josiah, Mr. - died 29 May 1850 at 53 yrs. 6 m.
   (A stone down and not readable, but GAR marker).
CARTER, Angie R. - died 13 Mar 1931 at 75 yrs.
   Joseph S. - son of Cornelius and Sarah A. Carter, died 14 Sep 1864 at 16 yrs. 6 m.
   Sarah A. - wife of Capt. C. Carter, died 10 Dec 1911 at 88 yrs.
   Cornelius, Capt. - died 2 Sep 1885 at 69 yrs.
ALEXANDER, James - died 7 Apr 1882 at 81 yrs.
   Elizabeth M. - wife of James Alexander, died 31 Aug 1855 at 45 yrs. 1 m.
   Melinda - died 31 Jan 1894 at 90 yrs. 2 m.
   Jennie F. - 1874-1935.
   H. Louise - 1880-1961.
   Charles H. - 1846-1929.
   Louise K. - his wife, 1850-1929.
   Hannah - wife of James Alexander (broken stone - no dates).
CORNISH, E. G. - 4 Dec 1811-8 Sep 1888.
   Abbie G. - 25 Aug 1848-30 Jul 1852.
   Elijah - 8 Sep 1839-12 Jul 1857.
   Minervilda - 22 Jul 1855-30 Mar 1862.
   Nathaniel - 15 Jan 1842-8 Aug 1876.
   Children of E. G. and A. G. Cornish.
   Catherine Abby - dau of E. G. and Abigail Cornish, died 29 Jul 1852 at 3 yrs. 11 m. 5 d.
The following Hogan, Gould and Beal inscriptions are on one lot:
HOGAN, Vincent M. - died 16 Dec 1879 at 51 yrs. 5 m. 14 d.
   Clara P. - wife of V M Hogan, died 13 Apr 1865 at 27 yrs. 8 m. 3 d.

Fannie J. - his wife, born 2 Feb 1832, died 14 Feb 1909.
Lilla - dau of V. M. & Clara P Hogan, died 7 Dec 1862 at 3 yrs. 5 m.
GOULD, Madorah A. - dau of Harrison A. & Mary E. Gould, died 7 Nov 1870 at 7 yrs. 3 m. 19 d.
Harrison A. - died 16 Jan 1864 at 28 yrs.
William D. - son of H. A & M. A. Gould, died 27 Sep 1866 at 6 yrs. 9 m.
BEAL, George H. P. - son of George & Martha A. Beal, drowned 2 Jun 1877 at 15 yrs. 8 m.
George - died 3 Mar 1911 at 79 yrs.
Mary E. - his wife, died 5 Sep 1901 at 60 yrs.
Martha A. - wife of George Beal, died 19 Sep 1866 at 32 yrs.
Dorah - only dau of Geo & Martha A Beal, died 15 Feb 1864 at 5 m.
Nathaniel A. - died 24 Apr 1908 at 78 yrs. (GAR marker).
Hannah E. - wife of Nathaniel A Beal, died 23 Sep 1867 at 36 yrs. 9 m.
Lydia E. - dau of N. A. & H. E. Beal, died 1 Oct 1858 at 1 yr. 8 m.
HUTCHINS, Joseph B. - son of A. D. & L. J. Hutchins, died 10 Apr 1886 at 24 yrs. 10 m.
CURRIER, Frank M. - 1860- .
Mary Elizabeth - his wife, 1869-1925.
SYLVESTER, Emma Bradley - 16 Jan 1853-22 Dec 1936.
ADAMS, Benj., Capt. - 1843-1930.
Cleora A. - his wife, 1846-1918.
Benj., Capt. - Lost at Sea, 1809-1866.
Lavinia - his wife, 1812-1891.
Thomas L. - 1851-1895.
HUTCHINS, Alexander D. - father, 29 Jan 1832-15 Sep 1899.
Lydia J. - his wife, mother, 2 Jul 1830-27 Jun 1902.

ALEXANDER, Lewis P. - died 27 Feb 1895 at 75 yrs. 1 m.
  Margaret M. - his wife, died 28 Aug 1910 at 88 yrs. 8 m.
  Fred J. - 1857-1934.
  Lettie P. - his wife, 1857-1946 (DAR marker and plaque which reads "Lettie P. Alexander Old Boston Chapter").
  P. Haley - 1837-1909.
  Kate M. - his wife, 1839-1919.
MERRIMAN, Mary J. - 1836-1919 (on back of Alexander stone with P. Haley & Kate M.).
(On back of Alexander stone, the following):
McMANUS, John - 1760-1843.
  Eliza - his wife, 1761-1844.
MERRIMAN, Henry, Capt. - 1803-1840.
  Catherine - his wife, 1804-1861.
  Charles S., Capt. - 1832-1873.
  John H. - 1831-1874.
MARSHALL, Chester M. - 1859-1937.
  Fannie Carr - his wife, 1866-1947.
POLLEY, Amasa - 1819-1906.   )On back of
  Mary E. - his wife, 1829-1913.)Frank
  Abbie T. - their dau, 1864-1887)Currier stone.
WILKINSON, Wm. - 1829-1897.
  Jane - his wife, 1829-1899.
DOUGHTY, Nathan - 1869-1955.
  Alice A. - 1864-1921.
HILL, Edith - 1886-1902.
STAPLES, Theodore - died 25 Mar 1889 at 88 yrs. 6 m.
  Miranda - his wife, died 9 Mar 1890 at 83 yrs.
SMALL, C. T. - 1847-1899.
  Sarah Alice Staples - his wife, 1843-1905.
ADAMS, Geo. W. - 17 May 1855-29 Jan 1934.
  Nora E. - 21 May 1860-1 Mar 1916.
  Wilber R. - 22 Jan 1880-30 Jan 1883.
  Charlie E. - 7 May 1883-19 Mar 1884.
  Ella B. - 9 Oct 1893-9 Feb 1894.

    Infant Son - 7 Oct 1897-9 Oct 1897.
STOVER, Urial - 1852-1933.
  Menirva A. - his wife, 1858-1918.
  Their children
  Charles E. L. - 1889-1892.
  Flossie B. - 1893-1894.
  Erenest W. - 1895-1895.
  Miles G. - 1896-1898.
  Alfred A. - 1885-1912.
SMITH, Alfred A. - 1854-1937.
  Hattie Stover - 1861-1895.
  Robert W. - 1892-1968.
  Ora M. - his wife, 1903-1967.
CLARK, Mary D. - mother, wife of Clinton H.
  Clark, died 30 Jun 1892 at 49 yrs.
COOMBS, Ella A. - wife of Daniel A Coombs, died
  31 Oct 1899 at 47 yrs.
  Verson D. - 1870-1941.
JAQUES, John S. - 1846-1915.
  Lucy S. - 1845-1931.
  Galen B. - 1871-   .
  Mary M. - 1820-1865.
  Mary M. - 1850-1865.
  Harmon - 1804-1877.
  Susan - 1813-1842.
  Priscilla - 1835-1839.
  Miranda - 1840-1844.
COOMBS, Francis B. - 1847-1929.
  Mary E. - his wife, 1853-1922.
  Minnie B. - 1871-1872.
  Benjamin P. - 1874-1956.
  Annie L. Card - his wife, 1876-1954.
  Edmund F. - 5 Sep 1901-1902, son of B P &
  A L Coombs (rest not readable as under ground).
CUNNINGHAM, John - 1848-1902.
  Lillian F. - 1853-1929.
  Harrison M. - 1888-1906.
  Violette - 1890-1915.

GILPATRICK, W. P. - 31 Jul 1882-7 Nov 1907.
BEAN, Amanda N. S. - 1841-1930.
  Colby - 1852-1921.
SKOLFIELD, Sarah, Mrs. - died 16 Mar 1854 at
  90 yrs.
MERRYMAN, Mary - wife of Thomas Merryman,
  died 20 Nov 1872 at 81yrs. 2 m.
  Thomas - died 10 Oct 1853 at 71 yrs.
MARSH, Roy L. - 1884-1949 (on stone of Nancy
  J. Marsh).
MARSHALL, Florence - dau of Mason H. & Ellen
  B. Marshall (no dates) (on stone of Mason &
  Ellen).
  Horace C. - 1899-1980.
  Flora Hatch - his wife, 1893-1947.
  Jessie Smith - his wife (no dates).
GILLPATRICK, Edmond H. - 1882-1965.
  Clarence - 1914-1917.
  Ralph - 1920-1920.
SETTLE, J. Alvin - 1909-1985.
  Margaret A. - 1914-1984.
COOMBS, Grace E. - (wife of Robert G. Coombs),
  1904-1980.
  Mark R. - son of Ernest & Louise Coombs, 20
  Mar 1955-26 Aug 1988.
TOWNE, June Estes - 1925-1975 (dau of David &
  Mary Estes).
SKELTON, James A. - son, 30 Mar 1943-10 Mar 1944.
GODDARD, Robert R., Jr.- son of Robert R. &
  Edith A. Goddard, 1924-   .
  Mildred M. - his wife, 1920-1991.
COOMBS, Ellen T. -1901-1987.
  George Mortimer - 16 Feb 1898-24 Dec 1975,
  SEA 1, U. S. Navy, World War I.
WEBBER, Eleanor S. - 1891-   .
  Frank L. - 1889-1965.
CHAMBERLAND, Ruth H. - 28 Oct 1920-13 Jul 1988.
  Robert L. - 17 May 1919-   .

UTECHT, Mabel D. - Navy Nurse Corps, World War I, 1888-1985.
HARRINGTON, Ernest C. - 1908-1973.
　Ruth M. - 1912- .
KIMBALL, Arthur A. - 1914-1973.
COOMBS, LaForest G. - father, 1898-1987.
　Beatrice L. - mother, 1907- .
CARTER, Kenneth L. - 1906- .
　Margaret M. - 1908-1976.
ROGERS, Patricia J. - 1932- .
　Ralph H. - 1928-1987.
McKENNEY, Florence E. - 1920-1988 (on a stone marked White).
SWANSON, R. Swantie - 6 Sep 1904-10 May 1970.
　Oscar - 12 Apr 1878-13 Nov 1946.
JOHANSSON, Matilda O. - 7 Mar 1879-29 Jul 1935 (on Swanson lot).
GIBBS, Melissa Ann - 1969-1982 (funeral home marker).
SMALL, Basil H. - 1914-1990 (son of Olive Small).
DOUGHTY, Jennie Beal - 11 Mar 1877-16 Mar 1977.
JOYCE, Stella Small (formerly wife of Timothy Small), 22 Nov 1884-19 Nov 1956.
McENTEE, Doland A. - 1905-1973.
　Beatrice M. - his wife, 1918- .
ADAMS, Laurence T. - 1922- .
　Geneva V. - his wife, 1928- .
　Their daughter
DAIGLE, Cheryl A. - wife of Raymond E. Daigle, 1951-1974.
UTECHT, Arthur G. - 1858-1923.
　Mary Spiess - 1857-1911.
　Mary E. - 1891-1961.
　Matilda F. - 1885-1981.
　Anna C. - 1 Nov 1897-2 Jan 1978.
　Hilmar P. - 7 Apr 1893-26 Sep 1987.
CARD, Shirley F. - 1920- .
　Robert T. - 1918-1986.
　Nancy L. - 8 Jan 1943-5 Nov 1991.

HART, Mary B. - 1893-1974.
STAPLES, Albert A. - son of George H. & Harriet
  I. Staples, 2 Jun 1891-6 Jul 1977.
CARR, Oscar L. - 6 Sep 1848-22 Aug 1853.
  Vincent H. - 24 Feb 1852-28 Jul 1853.
  John H. - 12 Feb 1857-25 Jul 1859.
  John V. - 26 Jun 1864-20 Feb 1907.
  Oscar L. - 15 Aug 1855-Lost at sea 1881.
  (Above Carr inscriptions are on Lemont Carr
  lot.)
RIDEOUT, Jacob, Jr. - died 23 Nov 1863 at 30
  yrs. 9 m. 20 d.
  Wm. Austin - son of J. & Martha W. Rideout,
  died 3 Mar 1858 at 9 m.
GILLESPIE, Martha W. - wife of Thomas Gillespie,
  Widow of Jacob Rideout, died 15 Nov 1871 at
  37 yrs. 11 d.
JAQUES, Alden P. - 1835-1909.
  Hattie Carr - his wife, 1837-1865.
  Marcia L. Avery - his wife, 1848-1897.
  Holman P. - his bro, 1845-1869.
DENHAM, Thomas - died 2 May 1879 at 82 yrs. 3 m.
  Marcia -wife of Thomas Denham, died 4 Jan
  1870 at 70 yrs. 6 m.
WHEELER, Wm. W. - died 18 Apr 1881 at 55 yrs.
  Martha C. - mother, wife of William W.
  Wheeler, 1828-1911.
  John W. - only child of William W. & Martha C.
  Wheeler, died 25 Mar 1858 at 11 m. 17 d.

  One sweet flower has bloomed and faded,
  One dear infant voice has fled.
  One sweet bud the grave has shaded.
  Our loved Willie now is dead.

  John C. - son of Wm. W. & Martha C. Wheeler,
  died 27 Jun 1890 at 22 yrs.
DOYLE, Abiz<u>ah</u> - died 21 Dec 1887 at 76 yrs.

Hannah - wife of Abizer Doyle, died 19 Jun 1898 at 79 yrs. 7 m. 27 d.

ROGERS, Alonzo - died 7 Nov 1878 at 62 yrs. (There is a GAR marker and flag. The stone has fallen.)

West Bowdoin Cemetery

HIGGINS, B. Franklin - died 1865 (no stone but in cemetery records).

INDEX

ABBOTT,106
ABELL,40
ACKLEY,92
ADAMS,3 4 6-8 15 35 44 45 51
 86 88 92 93 95 96 100 101
 137 147 149 150 152 167 168
 171
ADERTON,84 152
ALDERSON,152
ALEXANDER,5 7 12 26 35 150
 152 162 164 166 168
ALLARD,3
ALLEN,9 20 32 37 41 52 64 69
 71 72 75-77 83 104 108 122
 136 147 152
ALLISON,74
ALPHEUS,8
AMES,45 50
ANDERSON,54 70 110 152
ANDREWS,93 150
APPLEBY,76 77 153
ARMSTRONG,88
ARNDT,46
ARNO,38 45 48 50
AVERY,18
BAILEY,49 77
BAKER,92
BARD,44
BARNES,57 90
BARRETT,40

BARTLETT,1 59
BATCHELDER,36 68 80 150
BATCHELLOR,162 163
BATES,91
BEAL,55 98 140 153 166 167
BEAN,170
BENNETT,18
BENSON,17 35 56 153
BEOTE,58
BERNIER,59 60
BERRY,86 143 144 147 153
BIBBER,15 153 161 165
BICKFORD,1 25 26 46 50 58 122
 152 153
BICKMORE,89
BISHOP,76
BLAISDELL,46 50
BLAKE,133-135 142 164
BLANCHARD,90-92 153 162
BLICK,51 60
BLOOD,76
BOEW,120
BONIN,45
BOOBIER,28 61 153
BOOKER,24 29 36 64 147 153
BOOMER,133
BOWERS,7 8
BOWIE,32 97 153
BOYNTON,38
BRADLEY,164

BRANCH,76
BRANN,40 45
BRIDGES,148
BRIMIGION,7 67
BRIMIJOHN,109
BRIMIJON,21
BRIMINGION,147
BRIRY,80 119
BRITT,110
BROCKLEBANK,51
BROWN,8 13 24 71 102 103 148 153
BUBERE,61
BUBIER,28 36 47 61 126 127 147 150
BUKER,19 20 21 25 26 98 106 115-117 119 120 122 147 153
BURTON,50
BUTTERICK,58
BYRAS,58 59
BYRNE,70
CALL,3
CALLEN,59
CAMPBELL,2 16 22 23 25 33 115 120 153
CANHAM,29
CARD,12 16 24 43 44 46 47 55 56 75 76 148 163 169 171
CARR,6 9 11 12 18 75 98 137 139 153 160 163 164 172
CARTER,9 18 97 153 154 166 171
CARVER,72
CARVILL,80
CARY,13
CHAMBERLAND,170
CHANDLER,2 22 23 40 53
CHAPIN,7
CHASE,22 81 83 84 86 109 147 154
CHRISTOPHER,154

CHUCK,19
CLARK,48 52 169
CLAYTON,46
CLEVELAND,135
COBB,92
COFFIN,41
COLBY,12 154
COLE,21
COLEMAN,94
COLLINS,59
CONLEY,47
CONNOR,6 7
COOMBS,1 9 15-17 26 32 34 38 49 51 55 62 64 75 97 109 130 133 134 141 144 147-150 154 169-171
CORNISH,2 14 42 54 59 99 141 142 154 166
COSKERY,48 49 52
COTTON,5 37 57 154
COULOMBE,71
COX,30 31 54 68 73 77
CRAIG,45
CRAWFORD,136
CRIPPS,127
CROCKER,141
CROSS,73
CUNNINGHAM,169
CURRIER,13 44 167
CURTIS,1 28 38 45 47 50 52 68 70 71 88-90 93 97 119 154 164
DAIGLE,171
DALRYMPLE,46
DANA,60
DANFORTH,65 154
DARLING,45 71
DAVIS,46 91 93 134
DAY,68 146
DECOVIN,52 67
DEGOVIN,75

DELANEY, 54
DEMCHAK, 45
DENHAM, 6 34 35 172
DENNETT, 80 148 154
DENNISON, 18 77
DEYMORE, 18
DODGE, 96
DOHERTY, 43
DOUGHTY, 43 57 58 168 171
DOUGLAS, 154
DOUGLASS, 147
DOWNES, 46
DOYLE, 15 21 24 25 98 148 154 161 172 173
DREWITZ, 108
DUNHAM, 65
DUNLAP, 82 83
DUNN, 28 154
DURGIN, 1
DURICKO, 60
DYER, 42 154
EASTMAN, 6
EATON, 25 95 131 132 133 146
ELLINGWOOD, 47
ELLIOT, 7
ELLIOTT, 43 93 133
ELSEY, 149
ELWELL, 75 84 85
EMERSON, 18 154
EMOND, 51
ENNIS, 24
EPHRAIM, 130
ESTES, 2
FARMER, 7
FARNUM, 84
FARR, 46
FELDMAN, 60
FERRIES, 43
FERRIN, 148
FIEHRER, 13
FISHER, 35
FLAGG, 107 108 150

FOLSOM, 125
FOSTER, 79 119 124
FOWLER, 51 54 55
FRANCIS, 144
FRAZIER, 40
FREEMAN, 19 23 155
FREEZE, 148
FRENCH, 155
FRY, 52
FULLER, 155
GAGNE, 113 114
GAGNON, 57
GALLUSHA, 61
GALUSHA, 61
GARBOTZ, 45
GARDINER, 99 155
GARDNER, 33 98 99 147
GARLAND, 33 43
GARRITY, 118
GATCHELL, 65
GAUBERT, 98
GAUTHIER, 46
GAUVIN, 39
GETCHELL, 34 64 65 87
GIBBS, 171
GILBERT, 48
GILLESPIE, 36 49 76 172
GILLPATRICK, 170
GILPATRICK, 1 29 148 170
GIVEN, 3 56
GLIDDEN, 155
GODDARD, 2 70 170
GODING, 137 138
GOODRIDGE, 4
GOOLD, 61
GOSS, 42 49
GOULD, 31 70 155 166 167
GOVE, 89 91
GOWELL, 13 29 60 121 128 129
GRAVES, 88 89 131
GRAY, 52
GREENE, 47 48 50

GREENLEAF, 72
GREENWOOD, 69
GREGORY, 96
GROSS, 53
GROVER, 24 36 39 57 72 76 77 79 81 82 83 123 125 126 147 150 155 165
GUPTILL, 16
GUSTIN, 49
HAIGH, 50
HALL, 5 11 14 33 43 74 148 150 160 161 163 164
HAMILTON, 102
HAMSCOM, 82
HANSCOM, 150
HANSON, 5 149
HARKNESS, 74
HARLOW, 93
HARMON, 54
HARPSWELL, 149
HARRINGTON, 2 46 171
HART, 172
HARVEY, 1
HATCH, 19 97 170
HATHORN, 39
HAWKES, 4 97 116
HAWTHORNE, 8
HAYNES, 98 155
HEALY, 39 40 42 55 56 74
HEBB, 69
HICKS, 57
HIGGINS, 32 36-39 51 52 67 81 83 100 148 150 155 173
HILL, 55 168
HILTON, 6
HINCKLEY, 47
HINE, 96 155
HINKLEY, 5
HITINGLEY, 2
HOGAN, 8 22 165 166 167
HOLBROOK, 3 42 64 70 75 109 155

HOLYOKE, 100
HOPKINS, 98 148
HORN, 133
HORTON, 42
HUNT, 21 92
HUNTINGTON, 4 13 70 87
HUSTON, 46
HUTCHINS, 167
INGERSON, 46
JACK, 107 109 139 144 150
JACQUES, 127 128 141
JAQUES, 5 9 142 169 172
JASPER, 24
JELISON, 82
JENKINS, 35 62 148
JOHANSSON, 171
JOHNSON, 28 31
JOHNSTON, 47
JONES, 1 34 35 39 41 49 50 53 54 56 64 87 122 155
JORDAN, 53 135
JOY, 42
JOYCE, 4 171
KATULA, 44
KEAY, 54
KEENE, 44
KELLAM, 69
KELLEY, 39
KEMPTON, 101
KENDALL, 96
KENDRICK, 13
KENNEDY, 155
KIMBALL, 146 171
KIMBLER, 55
KING, 59
KNIGHT, 106 150 155
KNOWLTON, 135
LAMB, 48
LAMBERT, 60
LAMOREAU, 46
LANCASTER, 87 112
LANE, 166

LAPHAM,23
LAVALLEE,71
LEONARD,3 110 132 155 162
LESAN,35
LEWIS,3 20 21 69 100 123 124
 141 156
LIBBY,38 48
LIDBACK,58
LINCOLN,15
LITTLEFIELD,46
LONGLEY,101
LORD,88
LOTHROP,93
LOWELL,45 56
LUCE,110
LUNT,47 137
LYDSTON,82 83 85 86
LYDSTROM,78
MACKENZIE,48
MAHER,60
MALOON,66-69 156
MALOY,74
MANTER,57
MARINER,113
MARKHAM,69
MARR,29 50 74 156
MARRINER,156
MARSDEN,2 3
MARSH,13 170
MARSHALL,13 156 164 168 170
MARTIN,74
MASON,2 149
MAXWELL,27 55 83 108 150 156
MAYBERRY,143
MCENTEE,171
MCINTIRE,51 59
MCIVER,2 3 45
MCKENNEY,171
MCKINNEY,58 59
MCLEAN,9
MCLELLAN,144
MCMANUS,168

MEADER,156
MERRILL,4 45 59 70 144
MERRIMAN,5 7 12 17 68 143
 156 168
MERRYMAN,6 7 12 17 170
MESERVE,131
METCALF,142
MICHAUD,48
MILLAY,90 91
MILLIKEN,59
MINOTT,20 71
MITCHELL,4 19 57 69 148 162
MOLOON,66
MORGAN,46 71
MORNEAU,48
MORRILL,13
MORRISON,71
MOSELEY,13 164 165
MOSELY,164 165
MOUNTFORT,110 156
MUDGE,33 156
MUMFORD,52
MUNOY,156
NASON,40 48
NAY,48
NELSON,51 98 135 156
NICHOLS,14 150
NILES,63 65 98 101 117 150 156
NORRIS,98
NORTON,84
NOWELL,16 28 56 57 72
NOYES,27
NUTE,44
O'GRADY,53 156
O'KEEFE,155
OLDHAM,52
OLIVER,64 83 93 150
OWEN,58
PAINE,89
PARKER,30 31 44 46 57 70
 134
PARLIN,112 149

PARRIS,49
PARTON,141 142
PATRICK,60
PATTEN,92
PATTERSON,39 69 90 93 132 133 150 157
PELKEY,51
PELLETIER,42
PENNELL,14
PETTIPAS,47
PHINNEY,42
PIERCE,3 162
PLUMER,160
PLUMMER,3 14 17 29
POLLEY,9 49 114 157 168
POOL,65
POOLER,45 53 57
POORE,69
POTTER,2 4-9 11 15 40 41 54 87 89 96 119 120 148 157 162
POWERS,93 143
PRATT,82
PRESTON,17 72 108 157
PRINCE,43 53 59
PROUT,2 48 57 157
PULK,55
PURINGTON,5 27 45 57 113 149
PURINTON,29 30 33 55-57 91 97 101 127-130 132 135-137 148 157
PURVES,64
RANCOURT,59
RAND,52
RANDALL,31 88 112 113 128 131 132 148
RANKS,73 80 150
REED,30 41 55 59 92 115 148
REEVES,98
REID,20
REYNOLDS,43 55
RHOADES,135

RHODES,6
RICHARDSON,47
RIDEOUT,10 38 42 64 66 69 73 74 148 172
RIDLEY,21 80 84 85 91 93 98 99 108 148-151 157
RIGGS,83
RINES,46 87
RING,61 62 157
RINGROSE,60
RIVERS,157
ROBERTS,40 47 50 51 60 72 73 149
ROGER,157
ROGERS,2 9 11 99 101 143 157 171
ROLLISON,54
ROSS,17 157
ROWLAND,89 90 92 111
ROY,3
RUSSELL,59
SALLEY,29 51
SAMPSON,20 68 74
SARGENT,41
SAUNDERS,19
SAVAGE,59
SAWYER,39 42 60 146
SENIOR,18
SETTLE,1 170
SEWELL,3
SHAW,1 2 17 157
SHEEN,19
SHEPERD,148
SHEPHARD,33
SHEPPHARD,34
SHERIDAN,44
SHORETTE,51
SIMMONS,52
SINNETT,129
SKELTON,2 3 43 45 47 60 104 128 129 131 170

SKOLFIELD, 170
SMALL, 3 4 8 12 13 19-27 33 34 46 53 58 59 65-67 69-73 76 124 125 130 141 148 149 151 157 158 168 171
SMALLEY, 148
SMART, 148
SMITH, 11-13 19 23 33 53 104 105 107 142 169 170
SMULLEN, 43 145
SNELL, 53 72
SNOW, 14 15 96 97 100 148 149 151
SPEAR, 46 49 148
SPENCER, 3
SPIESS, 171
SPRINGER, 35 36 56
STAPLES, 8 15 16 168 172
STARBIRD, 56 71 80-84 86 92 115 138 139 148 149 151 158
STEELE, 158
STEVENS, 44
STEWART, 45 48 63 158
STINSON, 87
STONE, 57
STOREY, 43
STOVER, 43 55 74 161 169
STROUT, 164
STUART, 39 44 63
SUTHERLAND, 158
SWANSON, 171
SYLVESTER, 10 17 40 167
TARBOX, 107
TARR, 33 37 50 54 55 59 64 82 86 117 128 148 149 158
TAYLOR, 58
TEMPLE, 24 63 76 110-112 149 151
THOMAS, 68
THOMPSON, 10 11 25 27 28 30 31 38 43 99 100 142 149 158
THORN, 129 130

THURLOW, 81 109
TIBBETTS, 38 145 146
TOOTHAKER, 149
TOTMAN, 149
TOWLE, 50
TOWNE, 170
TOWNS, 120
TOWNSEND, 48 72 73 151
TRICH, 69
TRUFANT, 3 4 13 158 162 164
TUTTLE, 70 71
UNDERHILL, 96
UPHAM, 54
UTECHT, 2 171
VARNEY, 21 22 88 89 149 158
VARNUM, 79 100 158
VERNEY, 81
VERNON, 49
VESEY, 12
VICKERY, 68
WAGG, 47 48 70 77
WAKEFIELD, 41
WALES, 52
WALKER, 43 49 51
WALSH, 69
WARD, 46 59 118 119 158
WEBBER, 2 15 16 24 34 47 48 170
WELLMAN, 1
WELSCH, 46 60
WENTWORTH, 41 50
WEST, 19
WEYMOUTH, 144
WHEELER, 50 65 70 77 92 113 114 158 172
WHITE, 13 44 77 105 106 151 158
WHITING, 158
WHITNEY, 40 48 149
WHITTAKER, 71
WHITTEMORE, 10
WHITTEN, 107

WICKWIRE,6
WILKINSON,42 168
WILLIAMS,32 34 38 42 49-52 54
    56 58 88-95 120 126 127 133
    149 158 159
WILSON,4 15 19 73 98 107 132
    139 140 149 159 161
WOODARD,32
WOODBRY,121
WOODBURY,134

WOODCOCK,69
WOODS,46 59 97
WOODSUM,44
WOODWORTH,159 161
WOOSTER,149
WORKS,148
YEATON,17
YORK,35
YOUNG,58
ZAUNSKI,162

www.ingramcontent.com/pod-product-compliance
Lightning Source LLC
Chambersburg PA
CBHW051056160426